POLITICAL MIGRANTS

Hispanic Voters on the Move

How America's largest minority is
flipping conventional wisdom
on its head

Jim Robb

NumbersUSA
Arlington, Virginia

Political Migrants: Hispanic Voters on the Move
© 2022, Jim Robb. All rights reserved.

Published by NumbersUSA Education and Research Foundation

978-1-7379547-5-0 (hardcover)
978-1-7379547-3-6 (paperback)
978-1-7379547-4-3 (eBook)
Library of Congress Control Number: 2022916121

www.NumbersUSA.com

This book is intended to provide accurate information with regard to its subject matter and reflects the opinion and perspective of the author. However, in times of rapid change, ensuring all information provided is entirely accurate and up-to-date at all times is not always possible. Therefore, the author and publisher accept no responsibility for inaccuracies or omissions and specifically disclaim any liability, loss or risk, personal, professional or otherwise, which may be incurred as a consequence, directly or indirectly, of the use and/or application of any of the contents of this book.

Table of Contents

Chapter One

Some Say the World Will End In Fire, Some Say Ice

T he political world was upended in 2016 when the defection of a significant section of the White working class from the Democratic Party put Donald Trump in the White House. Today, a large portion of Hispanic voters seem to be embarking on the same journey into populist conservatism that so far seems certain to benefit the Republican party. Why are these Hispanics moving to a party that increasingly has been identified with calls for less illegal and legal immigration? Wasn't that supposed to drive them away? How much have Hispanic voters moved thus far? How far will the movement go? For Republicans, how can they exploit this shift to regain national power? For Democrats, what accommodations can they make to avoid losing another key demographic?

Everyone in politics is talking about this movement. In July 2022, *Axios* stated, "Shifts in the demographics of the two parties' supporters—taking place before our eyes—are arguably the biggest political story of our time."[1] Is it for real? How big is the shift? What are its causes? Will it continue into the upcoming 2022 Congressional midterm elections and then on into the future? Dozens of political analysts and specialized reporters who make their living poring over election and political survey results, putting their fingers into the air, and making educated guesses about what will happen next, have been busy examining and re-examining this subject since the results of the 2020 election came in.

Behind the talk there's some simple, but stark, math. There are 62 million Hispanics living in America as of 2020, up from 35.7 million who lived here in the year 2000. That's 74% growth in just 20 years. Hispanics are now closing in on being one-fifth of the U.S. population. The speed of this increase almost boggles the imagination, especially when you consider there were relatively few Hispanics in this country 50 years ago—only nine million! In this new century, Hispanics have surpassed Black Americans to become the largest ethnic minority group in the country.

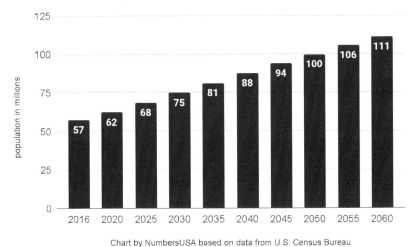

Forecast of the Hispanic Population of the United States

Chart by NumbersUSA based on data from U.S. Census Bureau

Fig. 1   Forecast of future Hispanic population of U.S.

But even these numbers seem modest compared to the projected size of the Hispanic population by the year 2060. According to the U.S. Census Bureau, unless government immigration policy changes, the Hispanic population will nearly double *again* by 2060, to about 111 million! That's more than the entire U.S. population during the first world war!

Of today's 62 million Hispanics in America, two-thirds were born here. Plus, almost eight million of the foreign-born Hispanic adults have been naturalized as citizens and are now eligible to vote.[2] In the 2020 presidential election, 16.6 million Hispanics did vote,[3] a rise of six million from the 2016 election.[4] That's 10.4% of the total votes cast. Put it another way, the Hispanic vote count increased 31% in just four years.

Yet this rapid rise in Hispanic voting seems low considering Hispanics are such a large segment of the population. Why the lag? For one thing, the average American Hispanic is only 29.8 years old, about nine years younger than the average American, and younger Americans vote at much lower rates than other Americans. Thirty-one percent of Hispanics are younger than 18—too young to vote. Another 14% or a bit more are illegal aliens. Six percent aren't allowed to vote because they are non-citizens—legal permanent residents or holders of a temporary visa. [5]

Even with those factors temporarily holding down the size of the Hispanic vote, young people will age, legal immigrants will become citizens, and many of those uninterested in the political process will be recruited to register and vote. Already in 2020, the Hispanic vote continued to close in on the Black vote in overall size—10% versus 12% for Blacks. What will it be in 2022? One study estimates that the percentage of eligible voters who are Hispanic will rise from 14% in 2020 to 19% by 2036. This seems reasonable, considering that this population will continue to increase rapidly due to natural increase and high rates of legal and illegal immigration.[6] (In a not-well-understood fact, many people who come to the U.S. illegally are able later to "adjust" their status and gain citizenship through one maneuver or another.)

No one knows how many of the newly eligible voters will actually turn out on election days, but it seems likely that between 15% and 17% of total voters in American elections might be Hispanic within 15 years, far outstripping Blacks in terms of voting power. The Hispanic population is huge and growing rapidly due to immigration. Every election over the next decades should feature a sharply higher number of Hispanic participants if immigration policies continue as is. And that number will represent an ever-higher percentage of the total vote.[7]

Who will they vote for?

Until very recently, it was assumed that Hispanic Americans would always tend strongly Democratic, save for a few special cases, such as Cuban immigrants in South Florida who were focused on resisting Castro's communist revolution, and perhaps recent arrivals from other

Latin America nations mauled by left-wing revolutions or revolutionary movements. The Hispanic allegiance to the Democratic Party is not hard to understand. Most newly established immigrant communities have voted for Democrats for two centuries. As the traditional party of outsiders, newcomers, and people needing a helping hand, the Democratic Party was the political embarkation point for Hispanics in America.

The results of the 2020 presidential election, plus the evidence of a myriad of political polls taken since the election (including a major poll commissioned just for this book), and also the results of a number of elections held since 2020, have forced just about everyone who studies politics for a living to agree that something potentially momentous is happening.

Hispanics are on the move politically. Unlike most Black Democrats, they seem unlikely to remain a predictable and endlessly patient voting bloc, frequently unhappy with positions taken by their party but too alienated from Republicans to contemplate a change. Instead, this vast population, so recently migrated from Spanish-speaking nations, is now involved in a POLITICAL MIGRATION. Where they end up, nobody can know for sure. But their political trajectory may be similar to several earlier immigrant groups, such as Italians, who after voting mostly Democratic for the first several decades, eventually stopped seeing themselves primarily as immigrants. When they made that transition, they started voting more Republican, which had always been the more immigration-restrictive party. Will the same thing happen to Hispanics? Many political analysts are pondering this question, and it is the subject of this book.

The political stakes could not be higher. Again, Axios stated in its July article, "Republicans are becoming more working class and a little more multiracial. Democrats are becoming more elite and a little more white. Democrats' hopes for retaining power rest on nonwhite voters remaining a reliable part of the party's coalition. Democrats' theory of the case collapses if Republicans make even incremental gains with those voters. Even small inroads with Hispanic voters could tip a number of Democratic-held swing seats to the GOP."[8]

Especially interesting has been the views of a group of middle-aged, Clinton-era Democratic political gurus who were around when the

White working class began to defect to the GOP in large numbers. They think they've seen all this before and are giving urgent warnings to their fellow party members.

The dean of this group is Ruy Teixeira, the Yale-educated expert on political demography[9] best known for co-authoring the 2002 book, *The Emerging Democratic Majority*. The book prophesied that the rapid growth of America's Hispanic and Asian populations, together with the steady relative decline of America's White working class population, would likely result within a few years in a long-term, sustainable Democratic voting majority.

Teixeira, and just about everybody else at the time, presumed that the new Hispanic and Asian voters who would join the electorate over the coming years would support Democratic candidates for office, just as earlier voters from those groups had tended to do. He had put it this way, "It is fair to assume that if Democrats can consistently take professionals by about 10 percent, working women by about 20 percent, keep 75 percent of the minority vote, and get close to an even split of white working class voters, they will have achieved a new Democratic majority."[10]

In the 2020 presidential election, indeed, although Biden and the Democrats again were terribly beaten among the White working class, earning just 33% of their votes, they greatly improved with the suburban voters (54%).[11] Most importantly, 73% of minority voters voted for Biden, not far off the 75% Teixeira predicted they'd need to win elections consistently.[12] But the *makeup* of Biden's 73% is what's causing alarm among Democrats.

Mitt Romney earned only 27% of the Hispanic vote in 2012,[13] and Donald Trump scored just 29% in his first campaign in 2016.[14] But after four years of border crackdowns and building the Wall, plus some shockingly ill-advised rhetoric from Trump about Mexican "rapists" and other criminals, Trump stunned everybody by gaining between 37% and 38% of Hispanic voters in 2020. Instead of driving Hispanic voters away, President Trump *attracted* many new Hispanic voters. To put this achievement in context, the 6+ million Hispanic votes Trump earned in 2020 is greater than the *total* number of votes cast by Hispanic voters for all candidates together in the 2000 presidential election, just two decades before.[15]

What's behind the shift?

I'll discuss more about Teixeira's famous prophecy, and why it did not play out as foreseen, in Chapter 3. I'll explore why the Hispanic population is dramatically different from America's traditional minority population (Black Americans) in history, outlook, and political self-image throughout this book, but especially in Chapter 8.

Today, Teixeira leads a small but vocal and influential group of Democratic analysts who are warning that Hispanics are slipping from their grasp right now, in the early years of the Biden administration. His *Substack* column, "The Democrats' Hispanic Voter Problem: It's Not As Bad As You Think—It's Worse," practically says it all:

"The Democrats are steadily losing ground with Hispanic voters. The seriousness of this problem tends to be underestimated in Democratic circles for a couple of reasons: (1) they don't realize how big the shift is; and (2) they don't realize how thoroughly it undermines the most influential Democratic theory of the case for building their coalition."[16] (That undermined theory, he might have added, was his own!)

Working class Whites began to shift toward the Republican Party around 1972, when so many voted to re-elect Richard Nixon, and even more shifted to the GOP when Ronald Reagan was first elected president. The movement of this group towards the GOP has continued, with some interruptions and hiccups, ever since. Famously, the huge swing of White working class voters in the upper Midwest toward Donald Trump in 2016 put him into the White House.[17]

Whereas 60% of Whites who are at least 25 years old lack a four-year college degree, among Hispanics this number is 81%.[18] A key thesis of this book is that the migration of the Hispanic voters, both working class and college graduates, into the Republican Party is not a unique phenomenon. Rather, it is the next and natural development in the movement of the White working class into a party that more closely aligns with the general policy priorities, social views, and cultural sensibilities of working people of all ethnicities in this country. Overall, the Hispanic vote-swing from the Democratic to the Republican column between 2016 to 2020 was eight points, with an even greater swing in certain Hispanic demographics. [19]

A massive amount of mostly Democratic Party-aligned research, which I will unpack in later chapters, suggests this shift is not a one-time fluke. And that the shift is being fueled by a general distaste for the progressive social and economic positions that are dominant in today's Democratic Party. One focus of this book is how many Hispanic voters are turning to the Republicans NOT IN SPITE OF the greater Republican emphasis on controlling immigration, but BECAUSE of this emphasis. Chapters 9 and 10 take deep dives into Hispanic attitudes on immigration and other issues as revealed by polls, including one specially commissioned for this book. They suggest that Democrats have mostly missed the mark with likely Hispanic voters by basing their aggressive immigration stance on mass amnesties, less enforcement, and higher levels of foreign workers.

The one point of majority Hispanic agreement with the Democratic immigration agenda is on a limited amnesty for perhaps two million so-called Dreamers who illegally crossed the border or overstayed visas as children. But the polling shows Hispanic voters to be deeply divided over the push to give lifetime work permits to millions more illegal immigrants of all ages. Overwhelming Hispanic voter agreement is found in the desire for *more* enforcement at the border rather than *less*, and for employers to be required to use E-Verify to keep illegal workers from getting jobs. Most Hispanic voters insist that employers claiming labor shortages should work harder to recruit non-working Americans rather than be allowed to bring in foreign workers, both lower and higher skilled. By 2-to-1 and higher margins, Hispanic voters want *lower* annual legal immigration rather than *higher* numbers, and to reduce annual numbers, they support ending immigration of relatives other than spouses and minor children.

Democrats, by shifting their immigration policies sharply toward post-national globalism in the 21st century, may have cost themselves the votes of not just one working class population, but of two.

What every thoughtful Democratic analyst has worried about is that the shift in Hispanic voting may prove long-term. In this book, I argue that Republicans may have a generational opportunity to position themselves as the party of working Americans of every ethnicity. Yet I'll also show that the Democratic Party can still compete for moderate Hispanic voters if it reacts to Hispanic defections by recommitting itself to more centrist positions on border security, employment, tight labor markets, safe streets, family-oriented economic policies, and an upbeat view of America.

One of my favorite poems is Robert Frost's playful-yet-serious "Fire and Ice." It begins, "Some say the world will end in fire, some say ice." The familiar lines seem to contrast a sudden and fiery, apocalyptic extinction of our planet to a gradual, colder, but just-as-certain ending by all warmth leaving and death coming on slowly. Like many of Frost's poems, readers are left to interpret the meaning of the verses as best they can. While some political movements, such as revolutions, can best be likened to the effects of fire, I think more great political movements can be compared to ice. It takes a while for ice to form, and you may not even notice it at first. But ice accumulates. It adds up. If it continues too long, you can think of literally nothing else but how cold it is.

If Hispanic moderate-to-conservative voters join the White working class in moving into the Republican Party, everything will alter for politics in America. Both parties will be forced to change, and change again. It will be a political migration that will carve a new American political landscape as sure as the Colorado River carved the Grand Canyon so long ago. The river flowed for millions of years to etch that wondrous place. Probably no one day seemed like much of a change. Over time, however, *everything* changed.

Chapter Two

Zoo Animals Go Crazy Just Before An Earthquake

On Election Night 2012, I sat at a desk amidst several of my colleagues in the conference room of our Arlington, Virginia headquarters analyzing the results of the Presidential and Congressional races for our viewers. We had turned our 11th-floor conference room into an impromptu TV studio with cameras and TV lights.

We were streaming a webcast to several thousand viewers interested in how the election results might affect U.S. immigration policy—our specialty. The biggest story that evening was President Obama's smashing reelection, as he easily stopped his Republican challenger Mitt Romney, picking up the usual critical battleground states of Ohio and Florida and going on to win 332 electoral college votes for the victory.

But the *second* biggest story that night came from the national Exit Polling run by the Edison Consortium for its television and other big media clients. Romney had won only 27% of the fast-growing, all-important Hispanic vote. Obama won 71% of Hispanic votes, and a second term.[20] This result was crushing for Republicans, since only eight years previously George W. Bush had earned a remarkable 40% share of the Hispanic votes in his reelection.[21] During the campaign, Romney had made a point to call for better control of the U.S.-Mexico border, and he'd rejected calls for a general amnesty of illegal immigrants, something George W. Bush had badly wanted to do. Romney's position was very popular with most Republicans.

President Obama, on the other hand, had said one of his biggest priorities for his second term would be to pass "comprehensive immigration reform," including more legal immigration and a general amnesty for the estimated 11 million illegal immigrants already residing in the U.S. "I'm confident we'll get done next year is *(sic)* immigration reform," Obama said in a campaign interview with the *Des Moines Register.* "And since this is off the record, I will just be very blunt. Should I win a second term, a big reason I will win a second term is because the Republican nominee and the Republican Party have so alienated the fastest-growing demographic group in the country, the Latino community."[22]

Whether or not the stark immigration policy differences were responsible, the 2012 election night results were showing that Romney had lost ground from Republican John McCain's already poor success with Hispanics in 2008.

"Hey, Roy," I said to Roy Beck, the president of NumbersUSA, my employer, sitting on the other side of the webcast table during a break. "The Republican Party is going to go into an absolute panic over these Hispanic results first thing in the morning." Another coworker there with us had been monitoring TV news all night. He said to me, "It's already started." And it had.

Sure enough, Romney's poor performance with Hispanics on election day was immediately cited by commentators as convincing evidence that advocating a more restrictive immigration policy was a political loser for Republicans.

In the days after the election, cable news featured a carousel of Republican wise heads who stated with absolute certainty that the GOP would have to change its immigration policy and much else or risk being buried under the rubble of a Hispanic voter earthquake in the future.

"If we don't do better with Hispanics, we'll be out of the White House forever," Republican strategist Ana Navarro, who had been John McCain's Hispanic co-chairman, said on CNN.[23]

It all reminded me of a *Washington Post* article I had read the year before, in 2011, about how the zoo animals went bonkers moments before a scary earthquake struck the National Zoo, and everything else in Washington. Iris, the usually unflappable orangutan, lost her cool, along with many other animals, a few seconds before the quake struck, knocking down stones on the Washington Monument and the National Cathedral, and cracking the glass on my home TV screen![24] Were the political pundits the zoo inmates of the hour? Was a political earthquake really about to shake the foundations of the Republican voting base?

A pessimistic autopsy report shakes things up

In March 2013 the Republican National Committee released its so-called autopsy report on the election loss, which predicted permanent underdog status for the party unless more minority voters, most especially Hispanics, could be enlisted. "We are not a policy committee, but among the steps Republicans take in the Hispanic community and beyond, we must embrace and champion comprehensive immigration reform. If we do not, our Party's appeal will continue to shrink to its core constituencies only," the report stated.[25]

It was a shocking revelation to the Republican Party's "core constituencies," who for more than a decade had opposed "comprehensive immigration reform." Legislation packaged under that title generally granted amnesty and lifetime work permits to millions of illegal aliens, greatly increased other importation of foreign workers, and promised – but did not guarantee – some extra enforcement to slow down future illegal immigration.

Reince Priebus, the energetic chairman of the RNC, championed the autopsy and its many recommendations, most of which were common-sense and overdue, like improving the party's digital outreach and hiring coordinators for outreach to various minority groups. More controversial, and what gained all the media attention, was the RNC's endorsement of a more expansive and permissive immigration policy. For this Priebus was lionized by media figures. Chris Cillizza and Sean Sullivan asked, "Can Reince Priebus save the Republican Party?"[26]

Personally, I wondered whether this panic was justified. After all, Mitt Romney, though an honorable, intelligent man, was burdened by a patrician manner and prone to awkward, off-the-cuff remarks. Recall, for example, the extremely insensitive and incautious statement he made to a group of donors during his campaign when he *thought* the cameras were not running: "There are 47 percent of the people who will vote for [President Obama] no matter what. All right, there are 47 percent who are with him, who are dependent upon government, who believe that they are victims, who believe the government has a responsibility to care for them, who believe that they are entitled to health care, to food, to housing, to you-name-it."[27]

Romney decidedly lacked a natural ability to connect with working class voters. On the other hand, Obama was genuinely popular, attracting a cult following among young voters, every minority group, and upper-income voters. He had a stirring speaking style that focused on the aspirations of Americans and personal glamor reminiscent of John F. Kennedy. Given all that, I wasn't too surprised Romney did poorly with Hispanic voters. Yet I strongly doubted Romney's poor showing amounted to a referendum on his immigration positions. In any case, I had little data to go on, so I put a mental question mark on the problem and carried on with my work of encouraging America to moderate immigration levels back to more traditional levels.

At NumbersUSA, we had our hands full stopping Congress from passing a big "Comprehensive Immigration Reform" bill that, astonishingly, would have nearly *tripled* the number of immigrants gaining lifetime work permits (green cards) during the first ten years after enactment. In the spring of 2013, America was still not fully recovered from the 2007–2008 "Great Recession," with a stubbornly high 7.5% unemployment rate. Many Republicans, still in panic over the previous year's presidential election loss and spooked by the RNC's autopsy report, turned their backs on the unemployed Americans and worked with Democrats to enact the so-called Senate Gang-of-Eight's bill.

Our specialty was activating hundreds of thousands of citizens to tell Congress exactly what they thought about impending legislation. Our activists, goaded by 250 million emails we sent to them in 2013, ordered over 4 million faxes to their representatives in Washington, placed tens of thousands of phone calls to Capitol Hill, and otherwise put the 535 members of Congress on notice. Many other things happened, but it's enough, for now, to say that the bill was quietly dropped by House Speaker John Boehner by the summer of 2014. The Senate-passed bill never came up for a vote in the House.

A year earlier, the Republican "autopsy" analysts and most news prognosticators were confident that the electorate was demanding an amnesty and immigration expansion legislation. Passage was often called "inevitable." But by mid-2014, that legislation was dead because enough Members of Congress feared that too much of the electorate was in fact *opposed*. Who was right about the voters' wishes?

KellyAnne's poll changes the conversation

In 2014, we asked KellyAnne Conway to produce a large poll to discover public opinion on immigration policy. In a couple of years, KellyAnne would begin her rocket ride to fame as one of Donald Trump's campaign managers, later to become a TV news fixture as Trump's most senior spokeswoman in the White House. Before all that, however, KellyAnne had made her name as a political pollster specializing in research of women's opinion. You could almost see the gears turn as she carefully weighed every sentence she spoke—an extremely impressive person. Sometimes on TV she seems a bit rehearsed, yet I considered her manner appropriately careful. Some of the results of her polls were startling.

In this poll for us, she asked respondents how many *legal* immigrants the United States should bring in every year. Since the poll was conducted using live telephone operators, respondents were asked to offer their own number that they thought would be best, and the operator just wrote that down. Of independent likely voters, those not attached to either major party, an unbelievable 47% volunteered that they thought ZERO legal immigrants per year was the best number for the country![28]

This certainly wasn't the policy goal of my group or of me. We preferred lower immigration numbers than today's rate, but still in the hundreds of thousands each year. I doubt many of the people polled *literally* desired to cut off all new foreign immigration. They probably weren't thinking of adopted children, or spouses of American citizens coming over, or persons needed in certain specialty jobs. But "ZERO?" It was obvious that the American swing voters wanted change, and not in the direction the Republican "autopsy" report had promoted.

What really got my attention in the poll was that 63% of *Hispanics* had agreed that Americans should be given the chance to take jobs now held by illegal immigrants! Again, I thought, how did Romney carry only 27% of the Hispanic vote when so many Hispanics evidently agreed with some of his key immigration positions? It was a mystery.

On June 16, 2015, commercial property developer turned TV reality star turned Republican politician Donald Trump glided down the escalator at Trump Tower in New York City accompanied by his wife Melania, to announce he would run for president. He had a big live audience waiting to hear his remarks, plus practically everybody in America who had a TV turned into cable news. My deputy, Suzanne, and I were two such viewers, watching from an office computer in Arlington. I remember my amazement when Trump promised to build a wall and have *Mexico* pay for it!

When we heard that, Suzanne and I turned and just stared at each other with, literally, mouths hanging open. Did Trump actually say that? For good or bad, an earthquake was coming. I could practically hear the orangutans scampering in their cages, the river otters banging into the glass, and the great cats flicking their tails as they looked for some way to get out.

A whiteboard debate at RNC headquarters

In December 2015, a few of us from NumbersUSA were invited to talk with RNC chieftain Reince Priebus and some of his people in the main conference room of the Republican National Committee headquarters. Our organization is open to talking with any party or candidate to show how they can help themselves by adopting immigration stances that are beneficial to American workers. The handsome, white stone RNC building is across the street from the three House of Representatives office buildings, and just a couple of blocks from the Capitol building. Nice digs!

Reince is an extremely pleasant and courteous Wisconsinite who greeted us smiling, sending staff out for beers while we chatted. He had an unusual way of communicating personal friendliness while also radiating skepticism about your views. We wanted to give him our ideas of how immigration policy might be a big factor in the coming year's Presidential election, and Reince was willing to let us give them. More than that, he was very engaged, asking lots of questions.

The thrust of our remarks was to convince him that his 2012 election autopsy report had been wrong in advocating permissiveness to illegal immigration, which we argued would lower, not raise, the Republican vote in 2016.

In response, the chairman got on his feet, grabbed a dry erase marker, and stalked to the whiteboard in the conference room. He wrote the names of the four big ethnic/racial voting groups and then their percentages of the overall vote in each of the past few elections. Clearly, the White percentage was going down while the Hispanic and Asian vote percentage was rising rapidly. Republicans' huge advantage with White voters could not reasonably get any higher than it already was, he suggested, while showing statistics of the party's rising majority percentages among Whites over a long period.

The only way for the party to win in the future, Reince said, was to focus on gaining ground with the other three groups that had increasing shares of the overall electorate, and Hispanics were their best target. That is what the autopsy report's pro-amnesty recommendation was supposed to accomplish. If immigration restrictionist stances blocked Republicans' efforts to make inroads with Hispanic voters then Republicans needed to avoid advocating those stances, or at least avoid talking about them. Of course, Reince was completely correct that the GOP badly needed to expand from its White voter base. But was he right about how to do it? Plus, was the chairman downplaying a real alienation among working class voters that had cost them support in 2012?

I remarked that his and the RNC's logic was flawed in two ways. I first had to remind him that we had a bunch of polls and other data demonstrating that it looked like a significant segment of the White working class had sat out the 2012 election. For example, the universally respected election analyst Sean Trende had written that population growth between 2008 and 2012 *should* have produced about 1.6 million more White votes (for all candidates) in the 2012 election. Instead, Trende pointed out, votes cast by Whites actually *declined* by over 4 million. Further analysis showed Trende that the voters who hadn't shown up on election day "were largely downscale, Northern, rural whites. In other words, H. Ross Perot voters."[29] Trende emphasized that the GOP had better figure out why Romney hadn't appealed to more White working class voters if it wanted to win elections.

From where I sat, White working class voters were highly motivated by policies like more security at the U.S.-Mexico border, mandating E-Verify for every employer, and lowering overall immigration numbers. That was the real message of KellyAnne's poll. The White working class was afraid of losing jobs to immigrants, I insisted. If you want the working class, you need to listen to them on this. It was difficult to see how Republicans could win back that group of stay-at-homes with a highly publicized amnesty push or looking the other way at continued illegal immigration. And in all likelihood, an amnesty push would cause many working class Whites who *had* voted in 2012 to sit out 2016.

The other major flaw was in misunderstanding the widely diverse Hispanic population. We had long pointed out that a far lower percentage of Hispanics vote for Republican candidates than answer polls favoring lower legal immigration and more immigration enforcement against illegal immigration. For example, Pulse Opinion ran a poll for us in 2013 that asked this question, "The U.S. Senate passed a bill this summer to raise the number of green cards for new immigrants from 10 million in the last decade to 20 million in the next decade. Do you support or oppose this increase?" Of the Hispanics who participated in the poll, 52% said they *opposed* the increase, compared with 42% who said they were in favor. When asked in the same poll, "Which do you agree with more: we have labor shortages that require increases in less-educated foreign workers, or there are plenty of unemployed less-educated Americans to fill the jobs?," 79% of Hispanics said there were plenty of Americans to fill those jobs.[30]

We were convinced that the Hispanic voters Republicans could attract most easily were those who agreed with White working class Republicans about the need for *more* immigration enforcement and *less* annual immigration. The RNC autopsy report, on the other hand, had advised trying to appeal to the Hispanic voters whose attitudes were the most *different* from the Republicans' working class base and with policies that would alienate that base.

As it turned out, most Republican candidates in the 2016 presidential primaries campaigned on immigration stances that appealed both to the party's working class base and to the Hispanic voters who shared the same views. The advice in the RNC autopsy seemed to be followed by few of the candidates, and none of the ones who followed the autopsy's immigration advice really gained a foothold. (Think *Jeb!*)

Although I admired Reince's energy and conviction, during our discussion I was thinking, "Reince doesn't get it. He thinks it's about lack of Republican voters' *loyalty*, but it's really about lack of loyalty of the party *TO* Republican voters." I piped up, "So, Reince, are you saying that the disenchantment of the White working class had nothing to do with Romney's loss?" He looked a little taken aback, but he replied, "No, I'm not saying that." But the meeting broke up a little while later with no real movement.

Trump finally outlasted Sen. Ted Cruz for the Republican nomination the spring following our meeting with Reince Priebus, and on November 8, 2016, he was elected our 45th President. How did he do that? Trump spent his entire campaign emphasizing two issues enormously popular with the White working class. Cracking down on illegal immigration, and getting tough with China on trade. Both issues hit home with voters because lousy trade deals had been responsible for millions of lost U.S. manufacturing jobs, and uncontrolled illegal immigration displaced American workers in blue collar jobs.

This time, the White working class did turn out! Boy, did they! Formerly, the northern, industrial (some call them "rust belt") states of Pennsylvania, Wisconsin, and Michigan had been called part of the Democratic "blue wall." That is, Democrats could count on these states to vote "D" in presidential years on and on. But on November 8, all three saw a surge in voting, and all three went for Trump, winning him the presidency.

Priebus' approach changed considerably since our meeting with him months before. He saw his way clear to accepting a more populist Republican worldview. He not only embraced Trump by the time of the nominating convention, but he also went with Trump to the White House to serve as his first chief of staff.

A footnote about Trump's election: Several months after Trump entered the White House, an article appeared in *The Atlantic Monthly* by Molly Ball, titled, "The Unsung Architect of Trumpism." Subtitle: "Kellyanne Conway's theory that Republicans could win a presidential election with an anti-immigration *(sic)* message had a major influence on Trump's platform—and his win."

"Conway's ideas were the key to a major shift in the way Trump addressed immigration, which became his signature issue," Ball wrote. The article cited a Conway poll that became a "pillar" of the "intellectual infrastructure of the populist movement" in which candidate Trump galvanized "working class white voters in Rust Belt states that had previously belonged to Democrats."[31] That "pillar" poll was the one we had commissioned. The article surprised us with the influence it assigned to the poll, although we had intended it to nail down how voters felt about immigration policy and to challenge the political establishment in both parties with the results.

But the article failed to note what may have been an even more impactful finding of our poll: Hispanic voters' opinions on most immigration issues weren't much different from that of the White working class. By large margins, the poll found Hispanic voters preferring big cuts in annual immigration and more enforcement against illegal immigration.

Those results kept us from being as shocked as many observers when analysts went over the 2016 election exit polling and found that, as insulting as Trump had often been in his comments about Hispanic immigrants, he didn't lose any of the Hispanic votes that Romney had won in 2012![32] In fact, he received a modest one percentage point more than Romney had gotten.[33]

Clearly, Hispanics were still leery of the Republican Party, but Trump's unnecessarily inflammatory rhetoric didn't chase away any more. At least 3.5 million Hispanic voters were still willing to vote for a president who said he would crack down hard on illegal immigration, even if he used insulting language. That fact and the findings about Hispanic immigration attitudes in our 2014 poll provided strong indicators for the shifts in Hispanic voting that would soon emerge.

Hispanics Wanting *Less* Immigration?

In 2018, Clinton-era Democratic pollster Mark Penn was running a well-designed poll of registered voters called the Harvard-Harris CAPS poll. It was sponsored by the Center for Advanced Politics at Harvard University, and I always regarded it as extremely credible and of high quality. In the January survey, Penn asked a question very similar to the one we had been asking for years in our polls about how many legal immigrants should come each year. What struck me was how Hispanics answered this question. While only 3% of Hispanics chose "none" for the best number, 30% chose the *next* lowest answer, "1 to less than 250,000." Another 22% selected "250,000 to less than 499,000." Added together, 55% of Hispanics wanted to cut legal immigration numbers by more than half! Seeing a Harvard University-backed poll getting similar answers to our own, made me more confident that we were on the right track.

A Republican backbencher in the U.S. House named Jeff Denham would have been well served if he had paid attention to those 2018 poll results instead of trying to appeal to Hispanics with expanded immigration and rewards for illegal immigration. That same year, he championed a Democratic bill that would have granted amnesty (work permits leading to U.S. citizenship) for the two million or so younger illegal immigrants who had been smuggled into the country as minors. This kind of bill has been called the "DREAM Act" or "DREAM Amnesty," and various alliances in Congress have been trying to pass it since 2001. Denham really stuck his neck out by going against his party leaders, who opposed it.

The bill has always failed so far. Polls consistently show widespread sympathy for illegal aliens who arrived as minors, but none of the efforts to legalize them up to that point included measures to protect children and minors from being put in precisely the same position as the so-called "DREAMers" down the road. Moreover, none of the various DREAM Acts included measures to protect the vulnerable American workers who would be competing with the amnesty recipients for jobs and wages. Our polling has consistently shown that Americans prefer any DREAM amnesty to include those protections.

Denham's Congressional district, California 10, was centered in Modesto, and the local economy depends on agriculture as its backbone. Currently, 42% of the district's population is Hispanic, and both parties have regularly won elections there. Denham had won in 2016 by only a few thousand votes. Apparently, he felt backing this DREAM bill would win him more Hispanic support.

I wondered whether Rep. Denham understood the true immigration policy views of the voters back home, *especially* Modesto's Hispanics. So, we commissioned Rasmussen Reports to drop a poll in the district and find out. The results came back with quite a twist. As Mark Krikorian wrote about the survey in *National Review*: "So if Denham is trying to save his own electoral skin at the price of splitting his party and helping elect Nancy Pelosi as Speaker again, then his approach to a 'Dreamer' amnesty must be super popular among the Hispanic voters he's trying to attract, right? Wrong."[34]

Krikorian was referring to the results of a question that asked views about the specifics of Denham's bill: "Would you support a bill that legalized certain young-adult illegal immigrants brought to the United States as children, but continued Chain Migration, kept total immigration at one million a year and allowed employers to hire without checking legal status with E-Verify?" Among Hispanic voters, only 38% said "Yes" while 50% answered "No." They were also asked the question about how many legal immigrants should Congress allow into the U.S. each year, specifying that one million was the current number brought in. Fifty percent of Hispanic voters said less than 250,000 per year, and another 11% said "500,000." Only 17% of district Hispanics favored legal immigration numbers higher than current policy.

Poor Jeff Denham alienated his party's leaders, and probably a good many Republicans in his district, by championing a Democratic immigration bill that most Hispanics in his district did not support! Sure enough, he lost his seat in the 2018 election. He's probably still confused.

I bring this personal chapter to a close now. The big swing in Hispanic voting in favor of Trump and the Republicans seen in 2020, and the many polls and other clear signals of Hispanic movement toward the GOP will be dealt with in subsequent chapters. My own focus has been on immigration, since that is my work. I know the immigration issue is just one of many issues that are alienating Hispanic voters toward the Democratic Party and pushing them to the right. It's probably somewhere down the list, with economic and social issues pulling more weight.

Yet the point for me is that Democrats—and many, many Republicans—have consistently deceived themselves into believing that by pushing more expansive, permissive immigration policies, they can earn the loyalty of the 62 million Hispanic Americans now and into the future. If that's what they think, they're not just wrong—they're dead wrong.

Both parties should pay attention to the zoo animals, who are again restless. An earthquake is coming. When it strikes, smart people won't be caught sheltering under stone buildings or hoary old illusions that are more likely to crush than protect them.

Chapter Three

'A Funny Thing Happened On The Way To The Emerging Democratic Majority'

In their dramatic political prophecy, *The Emerging Democratic Majority*, published in 2002, John Judis and Ruy Teixeira predicted that the Democratic Party would ride the demographic trend of ever more ethnic minority voters to a durable majority. "Democrats aren't there yet, but barring the unforeseen, they should arrive by the decade's end."[35]

Why were the authors so confident? After all, when they wrote their book, George W. Bush was in his first term, riding high from leading the country's stern reaction to the 9-11 terrorist attacks but had not yet involved America in the Iraq War. Republicans controlled the House of Representatives and were to gain control of the Senate later that year. The president's job approval hovered in the mid-60s for most of 2002.[36] The economy had recovered from the twin shocks of the dot com bust and 9-11 and was growing again. In general, things were going okay.

Yet underneath the relatively calm surface, Judis and Teixeira felt they could detect bigger, structural trends that would soon congeal to form a long-term Democratic electoral advantage in the near future. Instead of concentrating on the personalities and policies of the politicians and officeholders of the day, they focused on changing demographics plus the shifting allegiance of two large groups of voters. The two groups were professionals, "who included teachers, engineers, and nurses, had earlier been one of the most Republican groups, but started moving towards the Democrats in 1972 and, by 1988, had become solidly Democratic." They also noted that working women voters had also once been Republican-oriented but had shifted steadily toward the Democrats.

But it was the authors' emphasis on the importance of a second group, minority voters, to the "emerging Democratic majority" that caught the attention of politicos everywhere. They noted that "minority voters, including blacks, Hispanics, and Asians, who had been variously committed to the Democratic Party, became overwhelmingly Democratic in the 1990s, while expanding from about a tenth of the voting electorate in 1972 to almost a fifth in 2000." They noted that the Hispanic population had exploded in the last decades of the 20th century due to immigration.

Judis and Teixeira were confident enough to reduce their argument to a formula. They said, "it is fair to assume that if Democrats can consistently take professionals by about 10%, working women by about 20 percent, keep 75 percent of the minority vote, and get close to an even split of the white working class voters, they will have achieved a new Democratic majority."[37]

Now, that's a ton of "ifs," but for a time it did look like the tide of history was running in the direction the authors had predicted. For one thing, the huge growth of minorities in the population continued and has not slowed down as of this writing. Especially after the publication of *The Emerging Democratic Majority*, many political analysts took every report of the growth of Hispanics and Asians in America as further evidence the Republican Party's days were numbered.

Two years after the book came out, George W. Bush was decisively reelected, but Democrats mostly put that down as a temporary rally-round-the-flag response to the 9/11 attacks and Bush's titanic military response around the globe. America's invasion of Afghanistan proved popular with the public and, judging from the lack of additional large-scale terrorist attacks on the American mainland, seemed effective in smashing Osama Bin Laden's Al Qaeda terror network. The 2003 invasion of Iraq was more controversial from the first, relying on shaky intelligence about weapons of mass destruction to win over a wavering Congress and U.S. public. When American troops went in, the terror weapons were not found; indeed, they were determined to have been no more than a self-defeating bluff made by Iraqi dictator Saddam Hussein. Bush's popularity suffered but not fast or steep enough for him to lose the 2004 election. Bush's approval ratings, however, slid badly throughout his second term.

Voters decide to dump the Republicans

By 2006, it was clear voters wanted a very big change. In the midterm Congressional elections that November, Democrats won a smashing victory, taking control of the House of Representatives and effective control of the Senate, winning 49 seats and having two independent Senators caucus (vote) with them. Not a single Republican challenger beat an incumbent Democrat in the House or Senate. The winds of change were not just blowing, they were fairly howling.

In the last two years of George W. Bush's second term, voters became even more sour on Republicans. As the 2008 presidential election loomed, Illinois freshman Senator Barack Obama ran against Hillary Clinton for the Democratic nomination and squeaked by her after a very hard-fought primary season. Obama was clearly left-leaning— the *National Journal* had rated him the very most liberal Senator in the year 2007.[38] Obama emphasized that his multicultural and multiracial background would make him better suited than either the current President Bush or the GOP nominee Sen. John McCain to restore peaceful relations with the Islamic world. Obama had abundant political gifts, a calm and mainstream public persona, and a talent for soaring oratory that shifted many White voters to his column. Even many people who did not vote for him felt good that a Black American could finally rise to the top of our society.

On January 3, 2008, after winning the Iowa Democratic caucus, Obama said, "They said this day would never come. They said our sights were set too high. They said this country was too divided, too disillusioned to ever come together around a common purpose. But on this January night, at this defining moment in history, you have done what the cynics said we couldn't do."[39]

Disastrous and probably fatal for Republican hopes was the Wall Street meltdown that unfolded during the fall campaign. The ultimate source of the trouble was the deep involvement banks and other financial institutions had in subprime mortgage lending. Due to a combination of bank greed and government pressure to make housing loans to people who would have never qualified due to credit history, low incomes, or both, subprime loans proliferated in the first decade of the 21st century. Many eager borrowers took out subprime loans on houses they couldn't afford, assuming that the enormous runup in home prices would continue and they could "flip" the houses and make a certain profit. The party was over when the housing bubble burst in 2007. During this period, about 3.8 million families lost their homes to foreclosure,[40] which began tipping the economy into a steep recession, quickly named "The Great Recession," or as I eventually termed it privately, the "Permacession."

I remember when the housing crisis hit my working class neighborhood in Fairfax County, Virginia. Seemingly overnight, dozens of neat little tract houses sprouted "For Sale" signs. Many of these became empty as the families were turned out by the banks but no new buyers were found. I happened to be traveling overseas in late September 2008 when the stock market crashed, losing a quarter of its value in a few days. I remember logging in on the laptop I had lugged to Europe, seeing the market sink and sink and sink. I can tell you that it's beyond disturbing to see your nation rocked by crisis when you are far away. John McCain never really had a chance.

On election day, Obama carried 28 states, including Ohio, which is significant because no Republican has ever won the White House without winning that state. Additionally, Democrats picked up eight more Senate seats, which, counting the two independents who voted with them, a 60-vote, filibuster-proof majority.[41] In the House, Democrats won 258 seats, a huge majority. Forty-three percent of non-Hispanic White voters voted for Obama, a respectable showing for a Democrat.

But it was the huge turnout and sky-high 95% support from Black voters that elected him, plus 67% of Hispanics. The Hispanic share of the total vote went up to 9.7% from 7.6% just four years earlier. People noticed.

Democratic Party Share of Presidential Election Vote by Race and Year

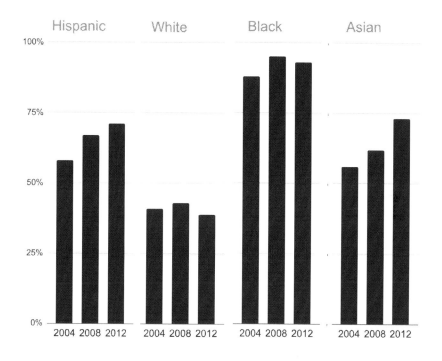

Source: Roper Center for Public Opinion Research, Pew Research Center

Fig. 2 Democratic Party share of the vote by race and year

President Obama governed a bit further to the left than he had run, and conservative Republicans fought his policies, especially the Affordable Care Act, dubbed "Obamacare," which Obama spent his first two years getting through Congress. By the 2010 midterm elections, resistance was fierce, and Republicans kept reminding voters that Obama had promised that "if you like your doctor, you can keep your doctor" under the new law, although that turned out to be untrue. The midterms were a rout, with Republicans winning back the House of Representatives. (They would have to be patient with the Senate, only regaining control of it in the 2014 midterms.) Chapter 2 of this book opens with what happened on Election Night 2012, when Obama overcame his lower share of the White vote (down to 39%) by gaining huge minority vote shares. As discussed, it was Romney's shocking

27% Hispanic vote share that created instant panic in the Republican chattering classes.

Democratic observers began to feel that Judis and Teixeira had been on target with their vision of a new and durable Democratic voting majority. Alan Abramowitz gave a paper to the American Political Science Association meeting in 2013 arguing that Judis and Teixeira had been dead-right. "Nonwhites and socially liberal voters were much more likely to identify with the Democratic Party than whites and socially conservative voters," the professor observed. "As a result, they were also much more likely to approve of the president's job performance and to vote for him. For example, according to the Gallup tracking poll, during the week of the 2012 presidential election, 78% of nonwhites approved of President Obama's job performance compared with only 40% of whites. These numbers almost perfectly matched the share of the vote that Mr. Obama received from these two groups."[42]

Painting with a broader brush, *Axios* ran a piece a few years later called "The GOP's demographic decay," which was mostly a chart showing the rapid growth of the non-White population in various states over the previous 17 years. Arizona had shifted from 36% non-White in 2000 to 44%, for example. Nevada had gone from 35% non-White to 49.5%. Florida from 35% to 45%. North Carolina moved from 30% to 36%. And Texas shifted from an already enormous minority population of 48% in the year 2000 to 57% by 2017. The article pronounced practically a final judgment: "There is no way Republicans can change birth rates or curb this trend—and there's not a single demographic megatrend that favors Republicans."[43]

One Democratic-leaning government professor at Harvard's Kennedy School, Thomas Patterson, enlarged on this theme with unintentionally comical effect in his 2020 book, *Is the Republican Party Destroying Itself?* In it, Patterson looks at all the demographic trends he says are moving against Republicans in recent years, specifically mentioning that minority voters are increasing every election, that new young voters are coming online, and he describes them as more liberal than their elders. He notes too that older White voters are in numerical decline. Organized religion is getting smaller, which he says will hurt the GOP since the religiously devout are often Republican, etc., etc.

Patterson touches specifically on Hispanic voters as it relates to his theory: "Republicans are paying a stiff price for defaming immigrants. If they hadn't, they could have made inroads with the Latinx population. Although most Latinx have conservative views on issues like abortion and national security, they vote more than 2 to 1 Democratic."

The author's diagnosis of a Republican Party nearly hopelessly behind numerous demographic and policy deficits gives him enough confidence to predict the long-term consequences for the party. He includes a chart of his design titled, "Projected Presidential Vote From Changes in Race, Ethnic, Religion, Education, and Generation (2018 Vote as Baseline)." He takes the two-party national vote share from the 2018 Presidential election and more or less straight-lines the Democratic vote share gaining in every future election through 2032, with the Republican share heading southward by the same margin. He imagines the GOP will earn no more than 41% of the national vote by the time of the 2032 election.[44] Tragic for Republicans if true. But is it true?

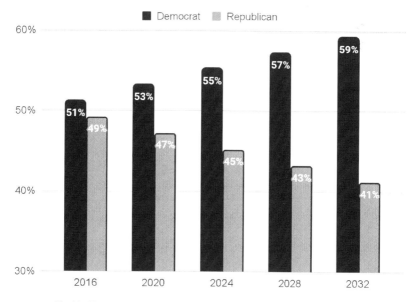

Chart by NumbersUSA, based on data from Thomas E. Patterson in the Boston Globe.

Fig. 3   Future president vote share projected by Thomas Patterson[45]

Now that we have the benefit of seeing his predictions falter in their very first election test, in 2020, Patterson's prediction seems almost a gross overstatement. While many younger people continue to be more liberal and Democratic-leaning than older voters, today's young voters will age and may well shift rightwards politically, as most generations have done over the past 100 years. Organized religion is experiencing some decline, but the remaining religious voters may adapt by moving to bloc voting. White voters may be in relative decline, but they may choose to respond to this fact by adopting more solidarity in voting patterns as Black Americans have done.

Overstating the case for demography is destiny

The left-leaning Center for American Progress also issued a report in 2013 called "Immigration Is Changing the Political Landscape in Key States." The authors of the study made no bones about the political cause-effect of demographic changes. "And as our nation moves toward a point where by 2043 we will have no clear racial or ethnic majority, 11 other states [in addition to California] such as Arizona, Texas, North Carolina, and even Georgia are also reaching demographic tipping points. Whether or not these states turn blue in the future has a lot to do with how politicians in both parties act and what they talk about on the subject of immigration reform." The authors believed that changes in the ethnic makeup of states, brought on by continued high levels of immigration, would likely turn the states reliably Democratic. This was all premised on the thought that Hispanics are much further to the left and much more connected to the Democratic Party than Whites.[46]

Another prominent voice in the demography-is-destiny school of thought is Steve Phillips, a former president of San Francisco's Board of Education and currently a senior fellow at the Center for American Progress. In his tome *Brown Is the New White*, Phillips confidently predicts a "New American Majority" emerging made up of White liberals and minority voters that will move the country dramatically to the left.

"Most leaders of the Democratic Party still operate under the mistaken belief that Republicans took control of Congress because White swing voters switched their allegiances to the Republican Party, resulting in the crushing losses in the midterm elections of 2010 and 2014," he states. "The real problem was lack of turnout of the Democratic base, but that analysis has not been done by the Party higher-ups, and hundreds of millions of dollars are being wasted in the futile pursuit of winning back White swing voters when a permanent progressive governing coalition could be established by investing those same millions in organizing the diverse communities that make up the New American Majority."[47]

Voices like Phillips have been influential in convincing Democratic party bosses that moving their party to the left politically is their best long-term chance of remaining in power. Maybe a third of Whites are progressive, this thinking goes, and that's enough *if* at least 75% of the ever-expanding population of ethnic minority voters could be counted on to back very liberal Democratic candidates. In other words, the party should place itself sharply to the left and let the country come to it.

Yet none of this works without Hispanics, who represented only 4.4% of the U.S. population 50 years ago and who represent 18.8% of it today. Will huge majorities of tomorrow's Hispanic voters be content to support Democratic candidates who take cutting-edge social stands like gender fluidity and no-limits abortion rights, together with support for wide-open international borders? Time will tell, but the trends of today's polling raise strong doubts. In a way, the entirety of the first 18 months of the Biden Administration could be considered an experiment on whether an unabashedly liberal Democratic government attracts or repels today's Hispanic voters.

Hispanics, the explosively growing group that must be factored into every political calculation of America's future, are decidedly *not* a monolithic, or even cohesive, ethnic block. Unlike Black Americans, Hispanic views and vote propensities are in rapid flux. (Much more on the differences in the experiences of Black and Hispanic Americans in Chapter 8.) They much more resemble political pilgrims than a political bloc, having come to a new country geographically, and now finding their way to political safe harbors as well.

Donald Trump's election in 2016 (as discussed in Chapter 2) immediately shook up most talk of permanent Democratic majorities, Patterson being a holdout. For one thing, Trump took 28% of the Hispanic vote in 2016, a point higher than Romney received four years earlier. Much more importantly, Clinton garnered just 66% of the Hispanic vote, down from Obama's 71% share in his reelection in 2012.

And as was discussed earlier, in his 2020 reelection bid, Trump significantly improved on his share of Black and especially Hispanic votes. The improvement among Hispanics was dramatic, with him gaining 37%-38% of their votes. That was still short of George W. Bush's 40% Hispanic vote share from 2004, but considering that the raw number of Hispanic voters had increased dramatically in only 12 years, and those new Hispanic voters had been predicted to be liberal and attached to the Democratic Party, Trump's improving record with Hispanics created something of a panic in Democratic circles.

Trump gained 8–9 percentage points with Hispanics in 2020 compared to 2016. If you combine that with the general shift Hispanic voters made away from Democrats, the gap between the two parties narrowed by 16 points in just four years—an enormous shift of Hispanics since 2016. Breaking the vote down by subgroups makes the scope of the change even more apparent. Pew's 2020 validated voter survey project determined that 53% of Hispanics with less than a high school diploma actually voted for Trump, as did 41% of the overall working class Hispanic group (less than a four-year college degree). Putting a metaphorical ice pick into the eye of analysts who confidently predicted that young Hispanics would be more liberal than their elders, Pew decided that it was Hispanic voters under 30 years of age who were the age group most likely to vote for Trump, at 41%.[48]

Jennifer Medina of *The New York Times* summed up the Democrat's predicament this way: "For years, many Democrats have presumed demography as destiny, believing that Latinos would come to vote for them with the same kind of consistency that Black voters do. A growing Latino population, they hoped, would transform the political landscape and give the party an edge in the Southwest."

"That dream ran into reality in this election," she continued, "in which the results confirmed what was evident from conversations with hundreds of Latino voters in dozens of settings from the early days of the Democratic primary until the long ballot-counting hours in Arizona over the last week: The Latino vote is deeply divided, and running as not-Trump was always going to be insufficient."[49]

That was two years ago, and there have been many developments since the last election to give Democrats more heartburn concerning where Hispanic voters are heading. Consider some polling data.

Polls show Hispanic voters unhappy with Democrats

Harvard-Harris CAPS

In March 2022, Harvard-Harris CAPS Poll, a poll run by Mark Penn, who headed up polling for various Clinton campaigns, partnering with Harvard University's Center for American Political Studies, released its new results. That month, only 35% of Hispanic participants thought the U.S. was on the "right track." 51% either "strongly" or "somewhat" disapproved of the job Joe Biden is doing as president. Fully 60% rated the U.S. economy as "weak." 49% said they had a "favorable" impression of Donald Trump. Their greatest concern right now? Inflation, at 33%. And get this—approval of the Republican Party: 51%. Of the Democratic Party: 50%. *Tied!*

In the upcoming midterm Congressional elections, which party are they likely to vote for? 44% said Republican, as against 56% who said Democratic.[50] Considering that the Republican Party has never actually received a 44% share of the Hispanic vote in the modern era, these polling results must have chilled Democrats to the bone.

Quinnipiac University Poll

The Quinnipiac University Poll, highly rated for its accuracy, in July 2022 asked this question, "If the election were today, would you want to see the Republican Party or the Democratic Party win control of the United States Senate?" Their Hispanic respondents chose the Republican Party by 45%, as opposed to 42% wanting Democrats to win control. When the poll asked Hispanics how satisfied they were with how Joe Biden is handling the economy, 72% said they *disapproved* of his handling, with only 19% said that they approved.[51]

In their May 2022 polling, Quinnipiac asked Hispanics whether they approved or disapproved of Biden's handling of "the situation at the Mexican border"? Thirty-one percent said they approved, but 54% said they did not. Overall, taking the two polls together, the Quinnipiac results strongly point to a restive Hispanic electorate clearly considering dumping their traditional political party—at least for this election cycle.[52]

The Wall Street Journal Poll

The *Wall Street Journal*'s new bipartisan-designed polling format issued more unpleasant news for Democrats concerning Hispanic voters in its December 2021 poll. It found that 37% of Hispanic voters said they would back Democrats for Congress in the November 2022 election, and 37% also stated they would vote GOP, with 22% not decided.

"'Latinos are more and more becoming swing voters.... They're a swing vote that we're going to have to fight for,' said Democratic pollster John Anzalone, whose company conducted the *Journal* survey along with the firm of Republican pollster Tony Fabrizio."[53] A later *Journal* poll in March 2022 actually put Republicans up by 9 percentage points among Hispanics.[54]

Morning Consult + Politico Poll

Democrats perhaps found some comfort in the April 2022 Morning Consult Poll produced by Politico, the wonky all-politics publication. Hispanics there said they would back Democrats over Republicans in the Fall 2022 election by 43% to 32%, with 27% undecided.

Balancing out that good news, however, Hispanics told poll-takers that they trusted Republicans in Congress more on the issue of the economy than they did Democrats in Congress, 41% to 36%. Approval of the job Pres. Biden is doing? Forty-four percent approved ("strongly" or "somewhat"), while 45% disapproved. Is the country on the right track or on the wrong track: 67% chose "wrong track." Who do Hispanics trust more on the issue of Inflation, Democrats in Congress or Republicans? Only 27% chose the Democrats, while 41% said Republicans in Congress. 32% weren't sure. The kicker was this question: "Now, thinking about your vote, what would you say is the top set of issues on your mind when you cast your vote for federal offices such as U.S. Senate or Congress?"

Respondents were shown seven groups of issues to choose from, including "Health Care Issues – like the 2010 health care law, Medicaid, other challenges." Other group clusters involved national security and "women's issues" like abortion and birth control. Not surprisingly, the issue cluster "Economic Issues – like taxes, wages, jobs, unemployment, and spending" got the nod as most important by 41% of Hispanics taking the poll. The next highest group, "Health Care Issues," got only 10% choosing it. (Women's issues got just 5%.)[55]

The New York Times / Siena College Poll

The New York Times runs an unusually small poll with partner Siena College, but sometimes they find interesting stuff. In their poll published on July 13, 2022, they talked with just 849 registered voters, so subgroups like Hispanics will have very high margins of error. Yet in this poll, they did find something interesting. "For the first time in a Times/Siena national survey," the accompanying article read, "Democrats had a larger share of support among white college graduates than among nonwhite voters—a striking indication of the shifting balance of political energy in the Democratic coalition."[56]

Only 41% of Hispanics in the poll said they plan to support Democrats for Congress in the fall 2020 election, with 38% said they would vote for Republicans. A huge group, 21%, were still undecided. Compare this to non-Hispanic Whites with college degrees, of whom 57% said they would vote for Democrats, as against 36% who said they would back Republicans, with 7% undecided. (For Whites as a whole, however, 37% stated they would vote for Democrats, 47% had decided to back Republicans, and 17% were undecided.)

This poll, which was conducted after the Supreme Court overturned Roe v. Wade with its Dodd decision, reflects a Democratic Party pickup among college-educated Whites. Yet, Hispanic voters showed continued drift *away* from Democratic loyalty. "The social liberalism of Democrats—on immigration, marijuana, L.G.B.T. rights, affirmative action, abortion and more—has simultaneously attracted progressive college graduates and repelled more culturally conservative working-class voters," wrote *Times* reporter David Leonhardt, explaining the poll results. "If you're trying to figure out why Latino voters have shifted right in the past few years, even during the Trump presidency, this dynamic offers an explanation."

Fox News National Poll

The Fox News Network is unabashedly conservative, but its polling operation has a reputation for rigor. *FiveThirtyEight* gives an "A" rating to the Fox polling, which is administered by Beacon Research and Shaw & Co. Research and uses live operators. Its May 2022 national poll had several interesting findings; Hispanic registered voters split on Biden job approval, with 51% approving and 48% disapproving the job he has done in office. When asked about Pres. Biden's job of handling the economy, judgment was more severe; 39% approved, and 58% disapproved. Biden's handling of inflation? Only 28% of Hispanics approved, with 66% disapproving on that score. On Joe Biden's job of handling immigration matters, 34% of Hispanics approved, while 56% did not. Finally, the crime issue was another area where Hispanic registered voters took a dim view of Biden's performance, with only 32% approving to 60% taking a negative view. The amazing thing is that Biden's overall approval was still 51%, considering that virtually every major issue had him under water.

On the generic ballot, the Fox poll had Hispanic ballots very narrowly favoring Democratic candidates for this fall over Republicans, 39%–37%, with a large 17% undecided.[57]

The Dallas Morning News—University of Texas at Tyler Poll

Most political polls offer breakouts of how Hispanics answer the questions. While this information is extremely important, the designs of most national polls make minority group results shaky and error-prone. That's because such a small number of Hispanics are usually included. If a poll is of around 1,000 registered voters, the usual minimum to assure good accuracy overall, the number of Hispanics questioned may only be around 150 or so. Due to how the magic of poll statistics works, the margin for error for such a small sub-group is pretty high. (Our own specialized poll of over 2,754 Hispanic likely voters has a tiny margin of error and asks some specialized questions not often addressed. It is discussed at length in Chapter 10.)

That's why I was so glad to see a poll of Texas registered voters that was conducted in May 2022.[58] Texas has a high number of Hispanic voters, so they actually interviewed 327 Texas Hispanic voters in the course of their research. The first interesting thing in the poll is the party lean of Texas Hispanics. While 58% either considered themselves Democrats or leaned to that party, 35% were Republican or leaned Republican, with 16% truly independent with no party lean.

This compared to 63% of non-Hispanic Whites who leaned GOP. So how did this group of party-balanced Texas Hispanics feel about important policy questions in early 2022? Problems for Democrats stand out immediately.

One possible trouble point for Democrats was that 47% of all Texas Hispanics stated that the Supreme Court *should* overturn the Roe v. Wade decision that legalized abortion nationally in January 1973 (and was overturned on June 24, 2022, well after the survey). The poll did not provide a breakout of how many Texas Hispanic Democrats wanted to axe Roe v. Wade, but the overall drift of the numbers in Texas should have made Democratic politicians cautious about using abortion as a wedge issue there.

Nonetheless, in a Democratic primary runoff in the Texas 28th Congressional District consisting of 77% Hispanics, Jessica Cisneros attempted to oust the moderate Democratic incumbent Rep. Henry Cuellar by centering her run on championing unlimited access to abortion. Cisneros was heavily backed by national progressive funders and also by politicians such as U.S. House "squad" leader Rep. Alexandria Cortez (D-NY) and Sen. Elizabeth Warren (D-MA), who were eager to end the career of Cuellar, sometimes called the last pro-life Democrat in Congress.

 Cisneros' campaign focus did very well in the northern urban edge of the district that includes parts of San Antonio. But what Henry Cuellar based *his* campaign on was border security in a district that lies primarily in the Rio Grande Valley. It was a decision that appeared critical to his very narrow victory. Many of Cuellar's campaign ads focused on his support of the Border Patrol and the need to stop the record number of uninvited foreign nationals pouring across the border. His campaign built on Cuellar's reputation since early in Pres. Biden's term of being the most outspoken Democrat in Congress in criticizing Biden's inability to maintain operational control on the Mexican border.

Cuellar's activism and choice of campaign focus was apparently the correct choice for his Hispanic district, according to a fascinating study by *Axios* published shortly before the runoff. The study tried to determine what issues were on voters' minds in various Congressional districts by studying what topics received the most Google searches. *Axios* found there were more searches on immigration and border issues in Texas 28 during the campaign than anything to do with any other issue, including abortion. Apparently, Cuellar had a firmer grasp than his challenger on his Hispanic voters' views. He won.[59]

During the month of the primary election, the University of Texas poll had found that only 37% of Texas Hispanics approved of Pres. Biden's immigration enforcement work on the state's massively long border with Mexico; 51% disapproved of how Biden was "handling immigration at the U.S. Mexico Border."[60]

I could quote many other polls. For the last year, almost every single one has been filled with alarming numbers for Democrats concerning Hispanic allegiance to their party. In Chapters 9 and 10, I lay out the findings of specialized Hispanic polling commissioned especially for this book. I believe these findings will clear up some of the mystery as to what is happening with Hispanic political movement.

I'll end this section on polling by citing an analysis of broad polling trends that ran in the *FiveThirtyEight* blog, the best source for public opinion poll analysis. In October 2021, the blog observed that "two groups with whom Biden has lost support stand out: independents and Hispanics. Independents have soured on Biden to the extent that his approval ratings among this group approach the strongly negative ratings they gave then-President Donald Trump at the same point in his presidency, while increased disapproval of Biden among Hispanics could signal they are moving further away from Democrats after they shifted somewhat toward Trump and the GOP last November,"[61] or maybe they just think Joe Biden is a uniquely ineffectual president. The blog included a chart (not pictured) showing the decline in Hispanic approval for Biden since his inauguration. Fig. 4, below, shows the steady rise in Biden *disapproval* among White, Black, and Hispanic adults.

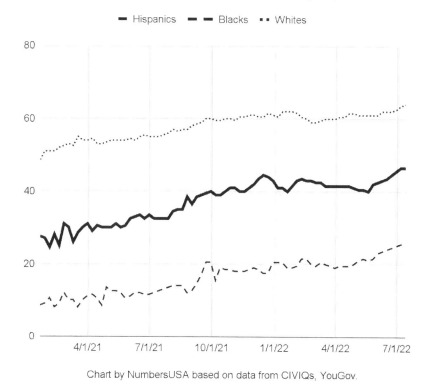

Biden disapproval ratings among racial/ethnic groups

— Hispanics ▬ ▬ Blacks • • Whites

Chart by NumbersUSA based on data from CIVIQs, YouGov.

Fig. 4 Biden loses more ground with Hispanics than with either White or Black voters[62]

Ruy Teixeira straightens out the record

Twenty years have passed since Judis and Teixeira wrote their influential book. In that time, they saw America elect our first Black president. Many saw Obama's election as proof that *The Emerging Democratic Majority* had already arrived. But they also witnessed the huge Democratic Congressional majorities be reversed and the presidential election and near-reelection of a decidedly anti-liberal Republican. To the shock of many observers, many more ethnic minority voters backed Trump the second time, after getting to know him, than had done so the first time. This was especially true of Hispanics who gave him approximately 2.3 million more votes in 2020 than in 2016.[63]

What did the authors think of all this? Were they surprised? No, not at all surprised. Ruy Teixeira, who publishes a substack blog called,

"The Liberal Patriot," is not surprised but he is disgusted at what he feels has been the Democratic Party's willful ignorance of his advice of 20 years ago. As *The New York Times* put it, "A funny thing happened on the way to the emerging Democratic majority. Twenty years on, the co-authors of a hugely influential work on the subject acknowledge that their party took a detour."[64]

It's true that Judis and Teixeira predicted that a coming realignment among voters could be wide-ranging and long-lasting, but the book did lay down a TON of conditions if the Democratic Party was to take advantage of these voting trends not only in the next few years but also on a more permanent basis. In the 2002 book, they said the mix of political issues that would win elections consistently for Democrats in the future was what they called "progressive centrism." Liberal, sure, but *moderately* so, concentrating on lunch pail issues attractive to working people. But after 20 years of seeing his party evolve, Teixeira wasn't satisfied they had understood his message.

"And even on this raw demographic basis, it's not crazy that there's a natural popular-vote Democratic majority in the country," Teixeira told the *Times*. "However, that does not translate into political power. We very specifically said [in the book]—and this is widely ignored—that for this majority to attain and exercise political power, you have to retain a significant fraction of the White working class. The country was changing, but it wasn't changing that fast."

Teixeira talked about a "professional-class hegemony" that "would tilt the Democrats so far to the left on sociocultural issues that it would actually make the Democratic Party significantly unattractive to working class voters." What kind of issues? Teixeira was specific.

"Go back to the 2020 Democratic primaries. It was remarkable the extent to which things that were alienating to the average voter, particularly your average working class voter, were gaily promulgated, with no apparent second thoughts about how it might appear to people outside the bubble. Things like open borders; basically, let's decriminalize the border. Anybody who knows anything about immigration and public opinion in the United States realizes that will not play well."

He also mentioned the perceptions that Democrats had become soft on crime, had become carried away with "this crusade against the superficial aspects of so-called systemic racism," and that their obsession with Fox News had blinded them to realities like the fact that many older black voters were actually conservative on social issues.

"It is difficult to avoid the conclusion that Democrats' emphasis on social and democracy issues, while catnip to some socially liberal, educated voters, leaves many working class and Hispanic voters cold," Teixeira observed in July. "Their concerns are more mundane and economically-driven."[65]

Teixeira is far from the only old-fashioned Democrat shouting warnings about his party driving away Hispanic voters. Thomas Edsall of *The New York Times* is also concerned. After the 2020 election revealed holes in Hispanic Democratic support, Edsall commented, "Although the Hispanic electorate is often treated as a bloc, it is by no means a monolith. It is, in fact, impossible to speak of 'the Hispanic vote'—in practice, it is variegated by region, by country of origin, by ideology, by how many generations have lived in the United States, by the depth of religiosity (and increasingly denomination), as well as a host of other factors."[66]

Edsall seemed especially concerned with the loss of Hispanic conservative voters. He cites Democratic pollster Joshua Estevan Ulibarri in building his case, reporting that Ulibarri told him that a growing number of Hispanics reject the label as "people of color," preferring to see themselves as White and rejecting the idea that they should vote with other minority groups. He says that whereas Hispanic conservatives used to vote Democratic because they considered themselves Hispanic first, conservatives second, and that Hispanics needed to stick together, that was now breaking down.

He quotes Ulibarri saying, "It is not just conservative men who have drifted away from Democrats. More and more younger people are identifying less with my party not because they are Republican or conservative, but because Democrats do not keep their word; Democrats are weak. And who wants to align with the weak?"

The *enfant terrible* of Democratic Party voter analysts is undoubtedly David Shor, who began work on Barack Obama's 2012 presidential campaign at age 20 and has variously entertained, informed, and horrified his fellow Democrats for the past few years with a constant stream of warnings to his party about alienating key voter groups. Shor had a lot to say about how Democrats began alienating Hispanics and other minority voters leading up to the 2020 election.

Like Teixeira and Edsall, Shor is alarmed about the cadre of young White progressive elites now controlling much of the Democratic Party's policies and messaging. Since the Black Lives Matter movement grabbed national attention in the late teens, Shor has tried to warn his party that many Hispanic *and* Black voters did not identify with much of their agenda. "The fundamental problem is that Democrats have been relying on the support of roughly 90 percent of Black voters and 70 percent of Hispanic voters," Shor calculated. "So if Democrats elevate issues or theories that a large minority of nonwhite voters reject, it's going to be hard to keep those margins. Because these issues are strongly correlated with ideology. And Black conservatives and Hispanic conservatives don't actually buy into a lot of these intellectual theories of racism. They often have a very different conception of how to help the Black or Hispanic community than liberals do."

Another Shor warning was specifically concerning Hispanics and immigration policy. According to Shor, Hispanics are wary of what Democrats are pushing. "In test after test that we've done with Hispanic voters, talking about immigration commonly sparks backlash: Asking voters whether they lean toward Biden and Trump, and then emphasizing the Democratic position on immigration, often caused Biden's share of support among Latino respondents to decline."[67]

A 2020 election post-mortem puts fear into Democrats

Many, many other Democrats have raised the alarm about the apparent hollowing out of Hispanic support for Democrats and how that threatens Democratic electoral hopes for the future. Perhaps the most searching and thorough such effort was prepared by EquisLabs, a research and activist Democratic group that amasses "ideas, innovation and leadership-development that has the potential to massively increase Latino electoral engagement and build long-term political power."

EquisLabs issued two post-mortem reports, in the form of PowerPoint slideshows, concerning Hispanics and the 2020 election. They're full of interesting information. One question many people have is why *more* Hispanics voted for Trump in 2020 than did in 2016 even after seeing his crackdown on illegal immigration at the U.S. Mexico border. Equis tries to answer this by showing that Hispanic registered voters gave low marks for Pres. Trump's immigration performance prior to the election but high marks for his work on the economy. One slide had the headline, "In 2020, immigration wasn't salient to vote choice— but approval of Trump on [the] economy was."[68]

Key findings include that newer, younger, female, and foreign-born voters were more likely to vote for Trump than other Hispanics. In a similar finding, *The New York Times* published a large-scale analysis shortly after the 2020 election that showed, using a series of charts, that the bulk of the extra votes cast in heavily Hispanic precincts in places like Chicago, New York, South Florida, and the Rio Grande Valley of Texas went to Trump.[69] The Democratic Party had worked very hard to get more Hispanics to the polls in 2020, and that effort paid off with a record turnout of 50% of eligible Hispanic voters casting ballots. This percentage is still less than that of non-Hispanic Whites and Blacks, but it was a big improvement over previous elections. The problem was that apparently many of the newly active voters pulled the lever for the other guy—Trump!

EquisLabs, in their postmortem, demonstrated that some of the newer, more marginal Hispanic voters were impressed by Trump's record of economic growth prior to the pandemic. In 2016, Equis found that Hispanics paid much more attention to then-candidate Trump's immigration positions and were leery of them. By 2020, however, concerns about immigration restrictions were not a big factor, but COVID restrictions were. For new and even formerly Democratic Hispanic voters, the study found, COVID restrictions such as shutting down businesses and schools, were associated with the Democratic Party and went over very badly among Hispanics. "Trump's policies on COVID and the economy were, in isolation, very popular— even among liberal Hispanics," slide 22 of the second post-mortem presentation states.

Among the most interesting parts of EquisLab's thoroughly interesting study was the poll they ran of 1,200 Hispanic voters who cast ballots in the 2020 election. They gave a series of issues that they said belonged to Trump's campaign, asking voters which ones they agreed with. *(See chart.)* Policies related to fighting COVID like "rapid vaccine development" and "reopen economy" got over two-thirds of voters' endorsement. "Middle class tax cuts" got 66% agreement and "get tough on China" seemed like good policy to 60%.

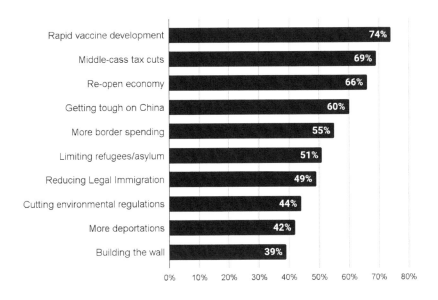

Chart by NumbersUSA based on data from Equis survey

Fig. 5 Hispanic approval of Trump administration policies

The immigration policies the poll asked about are the most interesting thing, however. "More border spending" had 55% of the voters in agreement, and limiting refugees and asylum got 51%. Even increasing the number of deportations gained 42% approval. "Build the wall," never very popular with Hispanics, managed to get 39% agreement.

All of those percentages were far higher than the 28% Hispanic vote for Romney in 2012 or the 31% for McCain in 2008. By taking those positions and advocating for them robustly, Trump tapped into a persuadable portion of Hispanics who never or rarely had voted for Republicans in the past, increasing his percentage of the Hispanic vote by 7–11 points over those GOP candidates. In fact, based on the high level of agreement with these key Trump priorities, it's a little surprising that Pres. Trump only got 38% of the votes of Hispanic Americans. His immigration policies were much more popular than that.

One voter quoted in the report put their attitude this way to Equis, "In the last elections, 2016, I didn't vote. For me I saw [Trump] as a clown. He's a clown... But he changed my mind. In my case, I felt a difference in stability. And he was running the country. Things that were problems [for] a long time, he came in and did something about them quickly at the beginning... He was doing things, not just talking about them."[70]

I think the most important finding of EquisLabs was how important the concepts of work and the American Dream are to Hispanic voters and, on the other hand, how off-putting socialism and socialist-like policies are to a demographic group thought to be overwhelmingly committed to the country's more liberal party. The lab asked 2020 Hispanic voters which of these they were more concerned about: "Democrats embracing socialism/leftist policies," or "Republicans embracing fascist/anti-democratic policies."

Nationally, 42% of Hispanics were more worried about Democrats embracing socialism, while 38% were more worried about Republicans and fascism. Not surprisingly, among the 2020 Trump Hispanic voters, 72% were more concerned about Democrats drifting toward socialism. From these kinds of numbers, again, it seems mildly surprising Trump's vote share wasn't even higher. Yet it is also a warning for Democrats of their risk if they allow the impression to remain or even grow stronger that their party considers socialism an acceptable model and socialist policies a real possibility for this country.

Chapter Four

What If Demography *Was* Destiny For The 2020 Election?

What Ruy Teixeira and all the other alarmed Democratic prognosticators are warning about seems to be centered on what they see happening next. For example, might Democrats lose the upcoming 2022 midterm elections because their immigration, crime, and other policies are just too liberal for a huge subgroup of Hispanics? (I'll examine this question using never-before-published polling later in this book.)

Demography—that is, the ethnic makeup of America's potential voters—was supposed to be destiny. An explosion in the number of presumably sympathetic minority voters was supposed to deliver the country perpetually into the hands of the Democratic Party. Yet Teixeira and many others came to doubt that this happy outcome would really come to pass. To sum up, these doubters are saying that the rosy predictions of 2002's *The Emerging Democratic Majority* have been undermined by unhelpful changes in the policies of the Democratic Party itself.

But ... BUT ... what if on the way to alienating too many Hispanics (and an uncertain number of Black and Asian and White working class voters), Judis and Teixeira's vision of demography being destiny was just right enough to deliver Joe Biden a very narrow electoral win in 2020. What if the growth in the Hispanic vote since the year 2000 in key swing states was indeed enough to create the margin of victory in this most disputed of all elections. In other words, even if the *percentage* of Hispanics voting for Democrats was declining, was the total *number* of Hispanic voters growing fast enough that the smaller-percentage majorities were producing larger *actual* numerical vote margins for the Democrats?

That's the possibility I began thinking about as my research for this book progressed. I certainly saw what the demographic nay-sayers were trying to communicate. The voices of caution were wary of a new young coterie of mostly White party officials, think tank mavens, and journalists educated at elite coastal universities. These more traditional observers were fearful that the young hyper-progressives were steering the Democratic Party away from its traditional emphasis on populist economic policies and toward policies and trendy causes that smacked of socialism, race hostility, and new alternative lifestyles to many traditionally Democratic voters. These traditionalists argued that most Hispanics and White working class voters did not care for concepts like defunding the police, giving up on defending our borders from illegal crossers, and district attorneys that did not prosecute serious crimes.

From the piles of statistical research I've studied about changing voter attitudes, I certainly agree it's likely that Hispanic voters, in particular, will continue shearing off from the Democratic Party as long as the party continues moving further left. But that's mostly about the future. Is there a chance that the changes in America's ethnic makeup, especially the enormous growth in Hispanic population and voting, have *already* changed the outcome of national elections?

I looked at the numbers, did the math, and I think I can say, "Yeah, the demographic change caused by continuing decades of mass immigration probably did win Joe Biden the presidency in 2020." Allow me to show you how. *(Follow along with the chart that appears in the Appendix.)*

Judis and Teixeira wrote their *The Emerging Democratic Majority* in 2002 utilizing data from recent elections, including George W. Bush's squeaker victory over Al Gore in 2000. Then, they examined Census Bureau projections of the growth of Hispanics and other ethnic minorities that would be making the American electorate younger, less White, and, they presumed, more liberal and Democratic Party-oriented. From all this, they predicted that their fellow Democrats would win regular victories in national elections by 2010 or so, and then on into the future.

We've already discussed what happened in some of these elections such as in 2008, when Barack Obama defeated John McCain, and in 2012, when Obama won a resounding reelection against Mitt Romney. We looked at 2016, when Donald Trump surprised the world by defeating Hillary Clinton. Finally, we analyzed the 2020 election, when Joe Biden won with a huge national popular vote majority. Yet, in '20, Biden won with only the narrowest of vote margins in four states that were necessary for him to receive the majority of what really elects a U.S. president: the electoral college vote.

In 2020, Biden won Georgia by only around 12,000 votes, Arizona by only 11,000, Nevada by just 34,000, and Pennsylvania by a relatively narrow 80,000.[71]

Georgia

The population of Georgia grew briskly (31%) in the two decades from 2000 to 2020, from 8.2 million to 10.7 million.[72] In the 2000 presidential election, Georgians cast 2,827,000 votes.[73] The 2020 election turnout reflected the state's population growth plus the huge rise in voter turnout, with 4,888,000 casting ballots.[74]

Now for the interesting part. Although the entire population of Georgia grew 31% in the two decades, the *Hispanic portion* of the population grew much faster. Of the 2,827,000 votes cast back in the 2000 election, only around 26,000 were by Hispanic voters, slightly less than 1%. Twenty years later, Hispanic voters cast 178,000 in Georgia's presidential election, a rise of 585% from 2000, and 3.6% of the total. Who did Georgia's Hispanic voters vote for? 62% of them voted for Biden, and 37% for Trump. Taking all the Biden votes and subtracting the Trump votes, it means that Biden carried the Hispanic vote in Georgia by a net 44,500 votes, well more than the 12,000 by which he won the whole state.[75]

(So, the way the math works is 178,000 * .62 = 110,360. From the 110,360 Biden votes, you subtract Trump's votes: 110,360—65,860 = 44,500.)

But here's the *really interesting and useful calculation.* (Remember, it's a thought experiment only.) What if the Hispanic vote in Georgia hadn't grown over 20 times faster than other groups? Rather, imagine that the Hispanic vote in Georgia grew only as fast as the other parts of the electorate grew. In other words, tons of non-Hispanic people moved to Georgia between 2000 and 2020, and a ton of them turned out to vote on November 8, 2020. What if the Hispanic portion of the vote had grown only as fast as the rest of it did? Instead of 178,000 Hispanic Georgians turning out in 2020 to vote, what if there had been only 44,000, which is how many there would have been if the Hispanic portion of the voters had only grown as fast as the other groups.

In *that* case, instead of Georgia Hispanics netting Biden 44,500 votes to help him carry the state, he would have only netted 6,500 Hispanic votes. Since Biden only won Georgia by 12,000 votes, a lack of the Hispanic population boom translating into votes at the polls would have sunk Biden in a must-win state.

Arizona

Similarly, Joe Biden only won the state of Arizona by 10,000 votes or so. It was very close. When Fox News projected that Biden would win Arizona late on election night, Trump officials and fans were furious because Trump had been leading until the votes from Maricopa County (Phoenix) came in. The 814,000 Hispanics who voted in Arizona in 2020 were 22% of the total. With 61% of the Hispanics voting for him, Biden netted 195,000 votes – way, WAY more votes than Biden needed to win. But what if Arizona's Hispanic voting had grown only as fast from 2000 to 2020 as the non-Hispanic portion of the electorate? In that case, only 501,000 votes would have been cast by Hispanics in Arizona, netting Biden 120,000 votes instead of the 195,000 net votes he in fact received. In this completely hypothetical, revisionist look at election history, Trump would have carried Arizona easily.

Nevada

To offer one more example, Nevada is a third key battleground state that would have moved from the Biden column to the Trump column if Nevada's Hispanic vote had grown between 2000 and 2020 only at the same rate as the other portions of the voting population. Instead of 239,000 Hispanic voters in 2020 in Nevada, there would have been in our hypothetical intellectual exercise much slower growth in Hispanic voting, and only 84,000 Hispanics would have voted. Instead of Biden netting 62,000 votes from Nevada's Hispanic citizens, he would have gained only 12,000. Result? Trump would have won.

Pennsylvania

The hill my thought exercise dies on is Pennsylvania, however. It's another state where Biden's margin of victory was pretty thin, only 81,000, which is just over 1% of the vote. That's close. Hispanic voters supplied 113,000 net votes to aid Biden. Remember, *net votes* means votes for your guy *minus* the votes cast for the other guy. Biden *netted* 113,000 votes of the 270,000 Hispanics who voted in Pennsylvania in 2020 (69% went for Biden and 27% went for Trump).

But if Pennsylvania's share of Hispanic votes had only grown slowly, as did the rest of Pennsylvania's voters, instead of 270,000 votes cast by Hispanics in 2020, there would have been only 90,000. If 69% had still gone to Biden and 27% to Trump, Biden would have netted just 38,000 votes from Hispanics. So, instead of winning the state by 81,000 votes, as he actually did, Biden would have to have settled for winning it by only 6,000 votes.

So, if the number of Hispanic voters between 2000 and 2020 had increased only as fast as other ethnic groups, Joe Biden would still have won the presidency, but only by a 6,000 vote margin in the one state he could not win without.

Biden's victory in that scenario would have been the closest presidential election in U.S. history. But because of continued high levels of immigration since 2000, the ethnic balance in fact shifted enough in Georgia, Arizona, and Nevada to provide Biden with a wide 74-vote victory margin in the electoral college.

But of course, all this is just a fanciful scenario to illustrate what may have happened if rapid immigration had *not* pushed up the Hispanic population in the early decades of the 20th century. I'm *not* saying history should have been different. Rather, I wondered just how right Judis and Teixeira had been when they speculated that changes in America's demographic makeup might by itself be enough to tip the political balance towards their Democratic Party. The exercise does seem to illustrate that they were onto something real.

The 45% solution—a much more sensible alternate scenario

Now imagine another speculative scenario that doesn't take as large a spreadsheet to calculate. Instead of using flights of fancy to play with the number of voters that *might* have been cast if immigration policy had differed, let's instead imagine something that could really take place one or two presidential elections from now.

What if America's Hispanic voters simply continue their shift away from the Democratic Party and towards the GOP? What if the trends seen in the last two presidential elections continue and perhaps accelerate? What if the answers Hispanics have been giving to political pollsters translate into actual votes at the ballot box in 2022, 2024, and beyond?

To find the answer to the impact of this imagined, more evenly divided Hispanic vote of the future, just for a minute, try changing recent history once again in your mind. Let's rerun the 2020 presidential election, and this time, try imagining that America's Hispanic citizens had given 45% of their votes to Donald Trump instead of the 37%-38% they actually did. What would that have changed about the outcome of the 2020 election? EVERYTHING!

With 45% of the Hispanic vote going to Trump and the rest going to Biden, Trump would have won Georgia by 14,921, taken Arizona by a rousing 103,503, squeaked by in Nevada by a margin of 4,240, and barely cleared Pennsylvania by 5,845. Trump would still be president now.

Can you imagine Republicans earning a 45% share of the Hispanic vote nationally? Remember, a May 2022 Quinnipiac poll referenced earlier found 47% of Hispanic adults saying they favored a Republican candidate for Congress over a Democratic one. Now, you know why so many Democrats are worried.[76]

Chapter Five

Why Hispanics Had To Immigrate To Get Into The United States

To better understand these Hispanic political trends and where they might go, we need to look a lot deeper at who these Hispanic voters are, where they've come from, and what their political history has been.

A big part of what makes Hispanic voters so interesting for our political future is how many there are, how many more there will be in just a few years, and how very little political thinkers seem to understand them. In Chapter 1, I placed a chart showing that the Census Bureau estimates the Hispanic population to grow from today's 62 million to 111 million by 2060.

The chart below shows just how rapidly the Hispanic population has already grown—so fast as to nearly boggle the imagination.

Seventy years ago, just after the end of World War II, there were just over two million Hispanics living in the U.S. As of 2022, there are 62 million. In other words, the U.S. Hispanic population has mushroomed almost *30 times* in just seven decades!

To put the number 62 million in perspective, think about the United Kingdom. That's England, Scotland, Wales, and Northern Ireland. Lots of Brits, right? Total population? 68 million. France? 67 million. Italy? Just 59 million. Maybe this will bring it home a little more for some. Our neighbor to the north, Canada, has only 38 million people. Within eight years the U.S. Hispanic population will be nearly *double* that of the entire Canadian population!

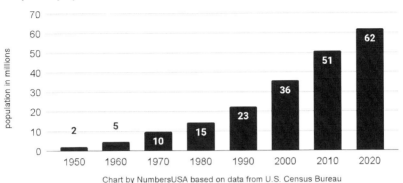

Fig. 6   Hispanic population growth from 1950 to 2020[77]

What does the term "Hispanic" even mean? This is surprisingly tricky to answer. The people we call "Hispanics" in the U.S. aren't really one people group. They come from more than 20 nations and territories that share the Spanish language and/or culture. They are White, they are Black, they are American Indian, they are mestizo and of other mixed races. Most—but far from all—speak Spanish with varying degrees of fluency. Though most relate to some Christian tradition, some are Jewish, some follow indigenous creeds, and a growing number claim no religion at all.

A fascinating study by Pew Research Center explains, "The most common approach to answering these questions is straightforward: Who is Hispanic? Anyone who says they are. And nobody who says they aren't."

For the most part, Hispanics are found only in the United States because "Hispanics" is a word adopted by the U.S. government, first appearing in the 1970 Census, as a catch-all term to cover the widely diverse population of residents described above. Spanish-speaking Guatemala, for example, is not filled with Hispanics. But its citizens become "Hispanics" in the eyes of the U.S. government when they move to the United States.

On the decennial (every 10 years) census, and in all the other census questionnaires the U.S. Census Bureau runs, the form first asks people what their race is. Then, *separately*, it asks if the person is Hispanic.

Below is the way the question appeared on the most recent Census form.

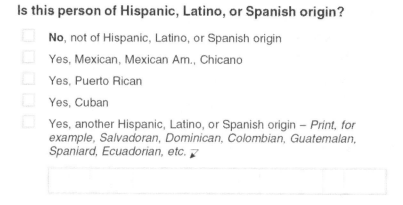

Is this person of Hispanic, Latino, or Spanish origin?

☐ **No**, not of Hispanic, Latino, or Spanish origin

☐ Yes, Mexican, Mexican Am., Chicano

☐ Yes, Puerto Rican

☐ Yes, Cuban

☐ Yes, another Hispanic, Latino, or Spanish origin – *Print, for example, Salvadoran, Dominican, Colombian, Guatemalan, Spaniard, Ecuadorian, etc.*

Fig. 7 Census Bureau form asking Hispanic origin

Since no U.S. law actually defines who Hispanics are, *self-reporting* is the rule. The interesting thing is that many people in America who are from families with roots in Spanish-speaking nations do not report themselves as such, and so they aren't counted as Hispanic.

Two-thirds were born in this country. That bears repeating. About 40 million Hispanics in the United States were born here, citizens at birth. The ancestors of some few of these settled here before there was even a United States. Others have come to this country only in the last few years. Some are wealthy, some are poor, and some are middle class. They include U.S. Senators and farm laborers. It's impossible to generalize. That's why in this book, we're going to use lots of numbers, charts, and statistics to build a picture for us.

In the beginning

Why has the federal government separated out Hispanics as a group different from other Americans, and why are they regarded as so distinct politically? After all, in several key ways, they are not unlike most other Americans. Like most White Americans, for example, most Hispanic Americans are at least partially of European descent. And the fact that the first American in most Hispanic families arrived in this country speaking a language other than English doesn't make them distinct, either. The majority of other American ancestors also arrived in the United States speaking a non-English language. Yet, there are cultural and historical reasons Hispanic voters as a whole might respond differently to various political issues.

We need a quick review of how the Europeans in the United States differed from, and interacted with, the Europeans in Latin America. Let's think back to the Americas before Columbus sailed here in 1492. There were two gigantic continents Europeans had never seen before,[78] but they weren't at all empty. Estimates vary wildly, but there were at least several million native people living in the Americas. There are no written records to tell us. Natives had built great empires in Peru (Incas) and Mexico (Aztecs), and several large confederacies of tribes in North America.

The Incan and Aztec empires were sophisticated. They mined gold, made metal weapons, built elaborate cities, and developed intricate government bodies. They were warlike, no pushovers militarily. But they were not a match for mounted, armored European soldiers with firearms, much less the new diseases the Europeans brought with them.

For about 100 years after Columbus found the Caribbean islands and claimed all the Americas for Spain, the Spanish and the Portuguese dominated European colonization, and they concentrated on South America and the Caribbean Islands. Gradually they expanded into Florida, parts of what is now Texas, California, and some of the territory in between. Eventually, the Spanish and Portuguese settled around a million Europeans in the New World. Additionally, they also brought in more than one million kidnapped slaves from Africa to work the fields. Many Indians were also enslaved and worked in mining and agriculture.

Beginning in the early 1600s, England and France also sent explorers and colonists to the Americas, concentrating their efforts in the Caribbean and Eastern North America. We all know that England planted 13 colonies that thrived along the eastern seaboard, in addition to colonizing various "sugar" islands in the Caribbean, including Jamaica and Barbados. The British came to stay, and more than a million British colonists came to America during the colonial period. By the time of the American Revolution, the population of the 13 colonies exceeded 2 million. Additionally, the British transported 3.1 million slaves to North America, but only 2.7 million arrived alive after their hellish passage in slave ships. Many of the slaves went to the islands and not the 13 colonies.

Diseases imported into the Americas, especially smallpox, wiped out the largest portion of the native Indian populations. The survivors lost control of their lands and were relegated to marginal areas or were assimilated over time.

The French sent many fewer settlers to North America. Many were trappers or traders, with fewer of them farmers than in the English colonies. They settled chiefly in Eastern Canada but also extended settlements into what is now the American Midwest and down to the port of New Orleans.

In the 1760s, war broke out between France and England over control of North America. In America, we call this the French and Indian War, but it was merely one theater of a larger, global war called the Seven Years' War that was fought by the two titanic powers of Europe. In the end, England decisively triumphed, ejecting the French government, if not the actual French people or culture, from Canada.

Chasing the French out of Canada caused England to run up a massive war debt. To help pay down this debt, the King's government was determined to begin direct taxation on its American colonists. That is, money collected from colonists in America was to be taken back to the mother country. (American colonists were largely self-governing and had always taxed themselves for their colonial government expenses.)

The colonists famously objected to the tax scheme on the grounds that they had no representatives in the British Parliament, and therefore they had no responsibility to pay for British government expenses. ("No taxation without representation!") It came to war, seven years of it. Fortunately for the Americans, the French wanted revenge for the loss of French Canada, and they sent soldiers and a navy to back up the Continental Army. In the end, General George Washington and his small army won the day.

The United States was formed. In 1803, France, under Napoleon Bonaparte, was facing yet another major war with Great Britain, and it needed cash. Also, with the British in firm control of the transatlantic trade routes, France had no real way to exploit its American territories. So, France sold the huge portion of land it claimed in the middle of North America, called the Louisiana Territory, to the United States for

$15 million, or just 3 cents an acre. That coup was followed up by the U.S. obtaining Florida from Spain in an 1819 treaty.

So, England continued to control Canada. The United States controlled much of the rest of North America. The map below shows the United States and its territories as of the year 1840.

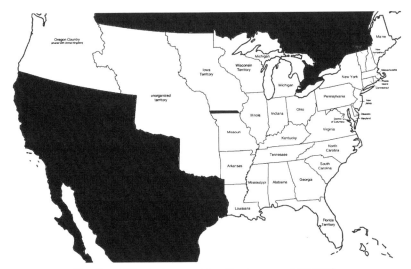

Fig. 8.   U.S. states and territories as of 1840.[79]

While France and Britain fought their endless wars in Europe and elsewhere for supremacy, Spain was undergoing a deep and permanent decline. The Spanish did not manage to use the massive treasure in gold taken from the new world to transform itself or its colonies into modern, productive economies. Poor economic performance led to military weakness. By the early 1800s, Spain lost control of its American colonies. By the second decade of the 19th century, revolution broke out throughout Latin America. Mexican residents began their revolution in 1810, and it took 11 years to gain independence. The areas of Mexico located in Central America did not wish to be included in Mexico, and they were allowed to form their own nations. Similarly, countries independent of Spain or Portugal were formed throughout South America

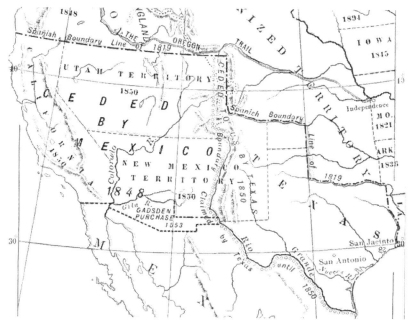

Fig. 9   United States lands deeded by Mexico to U.S.[80]

As you can see from the map above, territory first claimed by Spain, and then inherited by the new Mexican government, included not only the land it now occupies, but also parts or all of what is now Texas, California, Arizona, Utah, Nevada, New Mexico, and Colorado.

So which group are the 'real' immigrants to America?

Pretty often, Hispanic activists have noted that it is a miscarriage of justice that their people who move into the United States from Mexico, Central America, or other parts of Latin America are called immigrants when so much of the current United States was once under the political control of Spain, then Mexico. Which group is the immigrants? One recently published book summarizes it in the title: *The Border Crossed Us: The Case for Opening the US-Mexico Border.*[81]

There are a lot of ways to answer that question. One is that most people living in America are descended from immigrants. Even Native Americans migrated here thousands of years ago from Asia. Only the descendants of American slaves can rightly say they never immigrated—they were kidnapped and carried to these shores against their will. The real question is not *whether* Americans came originally from other places, but *when* they made those moves. Although Spain and Mexico claimed large portions of the American West until the mid-19th century, they never really populated it.

Mexico's 1821 population of 6.65 million[82] was not much less than the United States' 10.3 million.[83] The difference was that only about one percent of the Mexican population lived in the areas that are now part of the U.S.[84] That wasn't enough to wrest the land away from the fierce Indian tribes that dominated the Southern plains states, most especially the Comanches.

I spent much of my childhood in Abilene, Texas, a railroad town built in the 1880s as a stop for the Texas & Pacific Railroad (later absorbed into the Union Pacific Railroad), located between Ft. Worth and Midland. When I lived there in the 1960s and early 70s, Abilene had about 100,000 residents, three church-related colleges, lots of banks and independent oil drilling outfits, a small Black population, and an even smaller Hispanic one. Since one of the Comanche key hideouts was in nearby Buffalo Gap, no settlers dared live there until after the Indians were defeated. When settlers came, the Civil War was over, so no one was brought out to that arid place as a slave. Remarkably, when I think back on it, there were relatively few Hispanic people in Abilene when I was a boy. I never even tasted Mexican food until I was 10 or 11 years old. The Spanish language was rarely heard. The reason was simple: the same hostile Native American population that had kept out most White settlers also kept out Hispanics until the Comanches finally surrendered in 1875.[85]

In fact, American settlers were first brought into Texas to help quell the Comanches. Outside of their small strongholds in the Rio Grande Valley and the mission town of San Antonio, Indians had prevented much settlement by Mexican people. The Americans were used to fighting Indians. The newly formed Mexican government instructed the American settlers to free any slaves they brought with them and practice the Roman Catholic faith when they arrived. The Americans were willing to fight the Comanches, but they did not free their slaves nor did many practice Catholicism.

By 1834, over 30,000 U.S. citizens already lived in Texas, most of them just recently having emigrated into that part of Mexico and over-whelmingly outnumbering the 7,800 Spanish-descent Mexicans who were settled there.[86] The Mexican government, sensing trouble looming, tried to reassert control, but it was already too late. The American settlers soon rebelled against Mexico, and they won their independence after several months of fighting, surrounding Mexican president Santa Ana and his army at the Battle of San Jacinto in 1836. Although the new Republic of Texas was not recognized by Mexico nor invited yet to be an American state, U.S. settlers poured in from mostly southern states, bringing their slaves with them. By 1845, Texas already had 125,000 people, including 30,000 slaves, but very few people of Mexican heritage.

In 1845, the United States annexed Texas, and that, plus a boundary dispute, erupted into the Mexican-American War, a large-scale conflict with many bloody battles, all fought in Mexico. Many of the prominent American Army officers who would later lead both sides in the Civil War, such as Robert E. Lee and Ulysses S. Grant, first gained real battle experience in Mexico. After two years of grueling warfare, the American victory was total, and Mexico was forced to sign over all the lands shown on the map shown in *Figure 6* above in exchange for $15 million. Immediately after gaining these new territories, the United States started forming states and territories out of them. Again, hordes of American settlers poured in, eager to get cheap or free land. Of the small Mexican population in Texas at the time, some moved south out of the state while few additional Mexicans moved north into Texas.

California was also seized and annexed by the United States in 1848 at the conclusion of the Mexican-American War. It had only an estimated 6,500 White and Mestizo residents of Spanish descent at that time. The Indian population has been estimated at between 30,000—150,000. There were also a few hundred U.S. citizens there at the time of the changeover. But the very first year of American control, a huge vein of gold was discovered at Sutter's Mill, California, and the news caused a worldwide stampede of would-be prospectors and merchants to cross deserts and oceans to stake their claim.

Within two years, the U.S. Census counted 92,597 persons in California, excluding Native Americans. After 20 years of U.S. stewardship, by 1870, the non-Indian population stood at 560,247. Yet the Hispanic portion of that number was just 22,409, less than 4 percent of the total. They went from being the dominant non-indigenous group to being a tiny minority. Although Mexico had once owned territory that now made up much of the western United States, Hispanic people had never really occupied it... not until the mass immigration of the late-20th century.[87]

Chapter Six

Currents Are Complicated:
Who Are Hispanic Americans Today?

U nderstanding who Hispanics are takes time and more than a little bit of patience. Again, this is not a homogenous group. The word Hispanic itself is a one-size-fits-all moniker for an enormous population of American residents whose ancestry and/or language and/or culture have some connection with Spain. Here are some questions that show why getting your mind around who Hispanics are is so difficult.

Are all Hispanics descendants of people who came to the Americas from Spain?

Nope, not at all. Many Hispanics are largely descended from African slaves who were brought to Spanish colonies sometime in the past. Others are mainly of Indian heritage, not having many or perhaps any European genes. Still others have European ancestry, but those ancestors are not from Spain or Portugal. Many Hispanics in the U.S. are descended from Italian, German, French, or other nationalities that first immigrated to a Spanish-speaking country before finally settling in America.

Further, although more than half of Hispanics in America trace their roots to Mexico, other large groups are from Puerto Rico, a U.S. territory whose residents are all born U.S. citizens, Central America, South America, and various Caribbean islands, such as Cuba. *(See chart in Fig. 7 for the countries of origin for America's Hispanic population.)* It's important to remember that although Puerto Ricans who have moved to the 50 states are counted as part of the Hispanic population, they are not really immigrants, since Puerto Rico is a territory of the U.S.

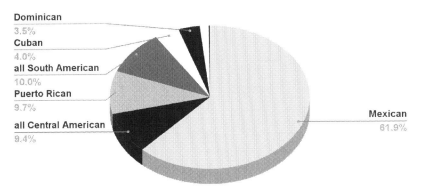

National origin of U.S. Hispanics

Dominican
3.5%
Cuban
4.0%
all South American
10.0%
Puerto Rican
9.7%
all Central American
9.4%
Mexican
61.9%

Chart by NumbersUSA based on data from U.S. Census Bureau

Fig. 10 National or territorial origin of U.S. Hispanics

Do all Hispanics speak Spanish?

No!! Fourteen million Hispanics, about a quarter of the total, speak only English in their homes. As of 2019, approximately 47% of *U.S.-born* Hispanics spoke only English at home.[88] Some Hispanic people speak no Spanish at all. Not surprisingly, the more time that passes between the original immigration experience of a family, the less Spanish is spoken. By the third generation in America, fewer than a quarter of Hispanics can really speak the Spanish language. But is knowledge of the Spanish language necessary to being Hispanic? No!! According to the Pew Research Center's rule of thumb, you're Hispanic if you call yourself such.[89]

Are Hispanics members of a particular race?

No!! "Hispanic" is not a term for a race. In fact, a growing number of Hispanics in America tell the Census Bureau they consider themselves White. A good example of this is the Rio Grande Valley region of Texas, that area in the southernmost tip of the state that touches the Rio Grande River and borders Mexico. The population there is 93.5% Hispanic, according to government data, but 88% of the residents also describe themselves as White, with another 9% calling themselves "some other race," and 1.4% saying that they are of two or more races.[90]

If this feels confusing, don't worry: Everyone is confused by it, including Hispanics! The government describes "Hispanic or Latino" as "a person of Cuban, Mexican, Puerto Rican, South or Central American or other Spanish culture or origin *regardless of race*"[91] (emphasis added). But if they don't all descend from Spanish or other European countries, and they're not of a particular race, how can you describe them?

"Throughout history, Latinos have been both colonized and colonizers," writes Geraldo Cadava. "By this, I don't mean simply the obvious: that Latinos are mestizos, the mixed-race descendants of Indigenous Americans, Spaniards, Middle Easterners, Africans, and other ethnic and racial groups. I also mean that Latinos have identified not only as survivors of imperialism and its ills, but also as supporters of imperial and national powers."[92]

Are Hispanics all Catholics?

No!! Although the Roman Catholic Church was the established state church of Spain and so held a virtual monopoly on religious expression in the Spanish Empire that settled most of Latin America, other faiths have been gaining strength in Latin America and amongst Hispanics in the United States over the past century.

A titanic 2014 study of religion among U.S. Hispanics found that 48% considered themselves Catholics, with another 25% belonging to a Protestant Christian church, most of these being Evangelicals. Additionally, one percent was Jewish. Twenty percent were unaffiliated with any religious group. Of these, two percent were Agnostic and another two percent were Atheist.[93] The religious affiliations of Hispanics are important in predicting their political alignment, as we will see later in Chapters 10 and 11, in explaining why some Hispanics are moving politically to more conservative party affiliations and voting patterns.

As was stated earlier in the book, two-thirds of Hispanics now residing in the U.S. were born in this country (including Puerto Ricans living here). About 20 million, however, are immigrants. Millions of these immigrated legally, usually by virtue of family categories commonly known as chain migration. However, at least 8.7 million either crossed the border illegally or overstayed visas to become illegal aliens.[94] Unless they receive some sort of citizenship-track amnesty, these individuals will not be eligible to vote. However, the federal practice automatically gives citizenship to the children of even illegal immigrants if they are born on U.S. soil.

The illegal alien population has been expanding very fast since Joe Biden became president in January 2021 and immediately began relaxing border security and asylum measures.[95] In fact, in the first 16 months of Pres. Biden's term, an estimated 1.35 million NEW illegal immigrants succeeded in evading border authorities, or were arrested at the border and then released on parole to travel and work inside the United States.[96] Most but certainly not all of these persons are of Hispanic heritage.

Because of legal and illegal immigration, the Hispanic population is currently increasing by more than one million a year. The Census Bureau projects that rate of increase to continue into the foreseeable future. A final question for this section is tricky.

Are all Hispanics in America *called* Hispanic?

NO!! Since the government and all other data-gathering entities use *self*-reporting to determine whether someone should be termed Hispanic, it gets much trickier to keep track as immigrants become children and grandchildren of immigrants. By the fourth generation in this country, only *half* of Hispanics are still willing to describe themselves as "Hispanic," although some of them might answer that they are of Hispanic heritage.[97] As assimilation does its wonderful work, many people just want to be known as Americans, but that will make counting the numbers harder and harder as time goes by.

Hispanics are a very young population: 31% are under 18, and only 7.7% are over 65.[98] That contrasts with the U.S. population as a whole which is 22.1% under 18[99] and 16% over 65.[100] And despite Hispanics' domination of immigration flows over the last half-century, it is a mistake to conclude that most Hispanics are foreign-born or that most immigrants are Hispanics. Only a third of Hispanics are foreign born, and only 40% of immigrants in this country are Hispanic. Of these, only about 35% came to this country illegally.[101] Nearly eight million of the Hispanic immigrants have already become U.S. citizens.[102]

Why did they come to America?

Hispanics have been present in what is now the United States since the beginning of the republic, but only in tiny, tiny numbers. As the chart on *Fig. 6* shows, most all Hispanics in America today come from immigrants who've arrived since the end of World War II. As stated earlier, a third of Hispanics are immigrants themselves. Of the two-thirds who were born here, most of their first American forbears have come since 1980. In general, America's Hispanics are a recently arrived immigrant group.

Why did Hispanics move to this country? In almost every case, it was to get jobs here. Yet unemployment rates are not currently sky-high in most countries the immigrants hailed from. Mexico's official unemployment rate in 2021 was only 4.4%. Honduras, 8.5%. El Salvador, 5.9%.[103] What gives?

Part of the answer is that immigration comes in waves. When a country finds itself in trouble because of natural disasters, like hurricanes as did several Central American nations periodically over the past few decades, or succumbs to civil war, as happened in both El Salvador and Nicaragua in the 1980s, or when security for normal people collapses as it has in parts of northern Mexico because of drug cartel mayhem being experienced right now, countries can temporarily become extremely hard to live and work in. One neighbor told me he decided to leave his native El Salvador for the U.S. during their civil war when rebel troops landed in his town by helicopter one day, and they began firing on civilian men of military age.

Those are the times many people choose to try another country within a relatively short period. During the 1980s, for example, half a million Salvadorans moved to the United States, most illegally.[104] Again, in 2001, when El Salvador suffered two large earthquakes, another big group left for north of the Rio Grande. But these setbacks in various nations are often temporary. Even today, with relatively good economic conditions, which translates into enough jobs for the local workforce, Central Americans and Mexicans still make the trip north. Why?

One argument is that Central America and various other Hispanic nations are perpetually violent places, that criminality there is committed on such a vast scale that living in those countries is equivalent to being in a war. A Doctors Without Borders study, for example, states that the "extreme levels of violence experienced by people fleeing from El Salvador, Honduras, and Guatemala, and underscores the need for adequate health care, support, and protection along the migration route through Mexico."[105]

How true is this? In 2018, El Salvador reported a murder rate of 52 per 100,000 residents. The equivalent figure for all of the United States for that year was 4.96.[106] So, 10 times higher in El Salvador. But most Salvadorans move to or near America's big cities where murder rates can be similarly horrific. In 2019, for example, the most murderous city in the United States was St. Louis, with 64.5 murders per 100,000 residents,[107] higher than any nation in Central America.[108]

Although migrants from Central America and Mexico are usually portrayed in American media as leaving countries full of miserable people, the World Happiness Report of 2022, powered by Gallup surveys, found the populations of those countries reporting a level of happiness that ranked in or near the top third of all nations. The widely referenced report ranked Honduras 58th, Nicaragua 54th, El Salvador 48th, Mexico 35th, and Guatemala 30th, just two spots below Italy. (The United States was ranked 19th, behind No. 16 Costa Rica.)[109]

The biggest draw of America has always been lots of high-paying jobs. Even if jobs can be found in sending countries, wages are much lower. In the United States, the average after-tax monthly salary is $3,619, whereas in Mexico it's only $628, and in El Salvador a mere $377 per month.[110] Of course, the cost of living is also amazingly higher in the U.S., so not all of the extra money made here results in higher living standards. Yet enough of the money earned in America can be saved and sent home that such "remittances" make up 23% of the entire Gross Domestic Product of El Salvador.[111]

Lots of hard work in hard U.S. jobs

What jobs do Hispanics do in America? Since we're talking about millions of individuals from more than 20 nations, and with two-thirds of them actually born here, obviously the answer is every job there is!

However, there are concentrations in certain industries. The Department of Labor says Hispanics hold 18% of all jobs in this country. That's up from only 8.5% just 30 years ago. Nationally, 35.7% of construction workers are Hispanic; 43% of those in "farming, fishing, and forestry" occupations have Hispanic heritage; Hispanics hold 37.9% of "buildings and grounds, cleaning and maintenance" jobs, and hold 27.3% of "food preparation and serving" jobs.[112]

On the East and West Coasts, and in states like Texas and Arizona, even those large numbers may feel low. Yet there are enormous swaths of the country with relatively low immigration where few Hispanics yet live. On the non-service industry side, 10.7% of all management positions are now held by Hispanic workers, a percentage that has doubled in the past two decades.

It's not surprising that Hispanics have become such an enormous slice of service sector jobs for several reasons:

1) **Incredible supply of young workers.** 62 million Hispanics currently live in America, and that's 18.7% of the population. Hispanics are about nine years younger than non-Hispanic Americans on average, so they are proportionally more likely to be in the labor force and also able to do the hard physical jobs best suited to younger workers.

2) **Less education than the average American resident.** As of the year 2016, only 16% of Hispanic adults had earned a 4-year college degree or higher, compared to 37% of Whites.[113] This means that the vast majority of Hispanic workers in this country are working class. (Again, the term "working class" is used only to refer to educational attainment, not to whether people hold jobs, etc. Working class simply means you have less education than a four-year college degree.) So not only are there tons of young Hispanic workers, fewer of them have the kind of education that leads to professional jobs.

3) **Lower wages among Hispanic immigrants.** As noted, two-thirds of America's Hispanics were born in this country, but a third moved here from less developed nations, all of whom feature sharply lower wages. As said above, Salvadoran wages are about 1/10th that of American wages. Immigrants from poor

countries may be more than willing to accept wages that are far less than that offered to native-born persons who may have held the jobs previously.[114]

4) **Illegal immigrants who often remain in low-level service sector jobs.** Of the perhaps 9 million Hispanic illegal immigrants in America, upward mobility is tough. To knowingly employ an illegal alien is itself illegal, so they often work in the service sector, sometimes being paid under the table. Most prestige jobs require vetting with the government's E-Verify system to check if the person is actually authorized to work in the United States.

That all said, America's Hispanic population is so vast that there are also millions of highly educated Hispanics working at the very top levels of their fields. Examples include Lin-Manuel Miranda, the *wunderkind* who brought the musical "Hamilton" to Broadway at age 35. Successful Hispanic politicians include Senator Ted Cruz of Texas. Supreme Court Associate Justice Sonia Sotomayor is obviously at the top of her field. Ellen Ochoa, a NASA astronaut, logged over 1,000 hours in space and was the 11th director of the Johnson Space Center in Houston.[115]

About 233,000 Hispanics were currently serving in America's armed forces in the year 2021. Twenty-three percent of the U.S. Marine Corps was of Hispanic heritage that year.[116] During the Afghanistan war, this included my nephew, Luke, a Peruvian native who served our nation as a Marine, winning a Purple Heart after being wounded in combat. (Luke fully recovered.)

The U.S.-Mexico border is a current and perennial security and law-and-order problem for our nation. As of this writing in mid-2022, more than 200,000 persons are being arrested each month as they attempt their illegal entry into the United States. Currently, the Biden administration is allowing more than half of these detained individuals to proceed into the interior of the country, often with work permits, cell phones and bus tickets, all courtesy of the U.S. taxpayer. This breakdown of order has become one of Pres. Biden's biggest political problems and is actually working to shift more Hispanics AWAY from Biden's party and toward Republicans. (Much more about this in Chapter 9.) Significantly, few realize that Hispanics are heavily represented in the U.S. Border Patrol ranks, making up about half of all agents serving.[117]

In several elite professions, however, Hispanics are severely under-represented. Only about 6.5% of U.S. doctors are Hispanic.[118] And only 8% of STEM workers (Science, Technology, Engineering, and Mathematics) are Hispanic.[119] The relatively short period of time that most Hispanic families have been in America probably accounts for some of this, since it has always taken time for most immigrant families to fully establish themselves in the country.

Considering that 19.3% of America's college students are of Hispanic heritage, however, a number in line with their overall share of the U.S. population, better days are ahead for Hispanic representation in good-paying jobs.

Chapter Seven

The History Of Hispanic Political Participation In The United States

Then most important single fact about Hispanics and the American political process was laid down in the Treaty of Guadalupe Hidalgo, signed on February 2, 1848, which ended the Mexican-American War. The treaty states that everyone living in the territories Mexico ceded to the U.S. after the war would be allowed to move to Mexico and still own their U.S. property. Or – and this is the key point – if they decided to remain in the U.S., they could choose to become full American citizens. Moreover, if they did not make a choice within a year but they stayed in the U.S., they would automatically become U.S. citizens.[120]

When bringing the former Mexican territories of Texas, California, New Mexico, Arizona, Nevada, Utah and Wyoming into the Union, American leaders wisely decided to eliminate future trouble by bringing the former Mexicans into the Union as well. Thus, the relatively few Hispanics living in the American Southwest were given full American rights. Now how could they benefit from them?

At first, it was very hard going, especially in Texas, where the Texas Rangers statewide mounted police force was slow to see people of Mexican heritage as fellow Americans rather than enemies after the Texas War of Independence from Mexico and then the Mexican-American War. The Rangers, who had become world-famous during the Mexican-American War with their fearless and deadly fighting methods, tended to be undisciplined, and this was to cause trouble off and on.

During the 1870s, for example, Mexican bandits frequently crossed the river into Texas and raided cattle ranches to rustle their livestock. Texas Rangers fought the bandits, not infrequently hanging suspected rustlers on the spot with no trial. The suspicion was that this vigilante version of justice was sometimes visited upon innocent Hispanic residents who happened to be at the wrong place at the wrong time.[121]

What happened in the Rio Grande Valley

Although there were relatively few Hispanics in this vast new American territory, there were pockets of settlement. One of them was in the Texas Rio Grande Valley, which is located at the southern tip of the state, nestled between the Gulf of Mexico and the Rio Grande River, which forms the border between Texas and Mexico. The city of Laredo had been founded in 1755 on both sides of the river, and the Mexican-American War divided the city in half. The first census of Laredo after the U.S. assumed control was in 1850. Census workers counted 1,173 inhabitants, mostly Hispanics. The population of Laredo was not large for the same reasons that other Mexican-American communities in Texas and elsewhere in the Southwest were small. The land was harsh and full of hostile Indians. By 1860, Laredo had only grown to 1,306, with only 21 being Anglos (the common name for Whites not of Hispanic heritage). Long-established Hispanics, often called Tejanos, owned land, voted, ran for office, and carried on as they had before the coming of the Americans.[122]

Nearby San Antonio, today a giant among Hispanic-majority cities in the United States, had only 3,168 residents in 1850.[123] The entire state had an 1850 population of 212,592, according to the census, of which 70% was White, 28% was Black, and only 2% were Hispanic or Native American.[124] The situation in New Mexico was different because it began life as an American state with a fairly heavy population of 61,587, most of whom were Hispanics. The 1850 Census found 80,000 former citizens of Mexico living in the United States in total.

After the Civil War, labor needs in the American Southwest and West began to be filled in part by Mexican citizens traveling north to work on farms. Some of these workers were seasonal, picking crops in season, then returning to Mexico to be with their families. Others became immigrants, however, and moved alone or with their families to the U.S. So, gradually the Hispanic population of Texas, California, and the rest of the Southwest began to rise. Yet the Hispanic population had only reached 500,000 by the year 1900, still only seven-tenths of one percent of the total U.S. population.[125]

Their small numbers kept Hispanic citizens from being much of a political force, except in those few areas where they were the dominant ethnic group, such as New Mexico, where many Hispanics were elected leaders. After the Civil War, American cities were frequently controlled by political bosses. Think of the Tammany machine that ran New York City's government. This system adapted well to border communities. In South Texas, Hispanics were the biggest group, and were both foot soldiers, voters, and leaders in a border version of big-city machines called "boss rule."

Because Republicans controlled the White House after the war, they also controlled federal patronage, doling out post office and other federal jobs to supporters even in Democratic strongholds like Texas. Using the same party colors as the 21st century, Republicans on the border organized Red Clubs to forward local party control, and Democrats created Blue Clubs. Like all boss governments, county jobs were handed out to supporters, and these petty officials reciprocated by turning out voters. In this way, Democrats and Republicans alternated control of South Texas border counties.[126]

I became aware of the old boss rule when I visited Starr County during a tour of the Texas-Mexico border in South Texas in April 2022. In one particular meeting with area Republican activists, I was asked if I had heard of the book, *Boss Rule in South Texas*. I said I hadn't but I would get it. The person recommending the book said the current struggle he and fellow Republican Party members were experiencing in trying to elect county officials and to send a Republican to Congress was not like that found elsewhere in the country. It was not primarily an ideological struggle between competing national policies and political ideas. Rather, he said, he and his fellow local Republicans were attempting to dislodge a Democratic Party "boss" machine that had run his county like a fiefdom for generations.

New Mexico and Arizona were U.S. territories for decades, only being admitted as states in 1910 and 1912, respectively. The President in Washington appointed the territorial governors, and they were almost always Anglos. However, Hispanics formed a majority of the populations in the years following U.S. control in both territories. That gradually changed as more non-Hispanic families moved in from elsewhere in America, and Hispanics went to minority status.[127] All this time, Hispanics in these areas were able to vote, did vote, were able to hold office, and did hold office. Wealthier, land-owning Hispanic families tracing their roots to the Spanish (as opposed to Mexican) era worked with Anglo newcomers to run things. In New Mexico, a Republican Party-oriented political machine called the "Santa Fe Ring" – a partnership of Anglo business interests and Hispanic families – controlled territorial politics during the last decades of the 19th century.[128]

A revolution in Mexico spills into the U.S.

Events from outside the U.S. soon made Hispanic political participation here more tumultuous, and far more ugly and violent. In 1910, Mexico erupted into a ten-year civil war known as the Mexican Revolution. I will not frustrate my readers by delving deeply into the internal politics, military campaigns, assassinations, failed and successful *coup d'etats*, and general bloodiness, but some key points should be understood.

First, the revolution happened in response to the actions of Mexico's President Porfirio Díaz, who had served various terms between 1876 and 1911. During that time, he defrauded Mexico's peasants by forcing them off of their land and then selling it to wealthy families. Millions of peasants had to go to work for the people who had taken land from them. Elections were held but rigged. The army and police were agents of oppression. The country was totally corrupt and unjust. So, in 1910, war broke out, and Díaz went into exile. But that was just the beginning of the trouble. Several rival armies arose. There were pitched battles. There was guerrilla warfare. There were assassinations and massacres. A string of leaders rose up competing for supreme power. The chaos was so great that nobody really knows how many Mexicans died of hunger, disease, and battle during the struggle. Estimates vary from several hundred thousand to the low millions.[129] By 1920, order was restored, but even today Mexican governments have not escaped their reputation for corruption. The Revolution altered government forms and gave Mexico a new constitution, but it did not bring about clean, responsible government for Mexico's people.

The second important thing to know about the Mexican Revolution is that it caused a large-scale out-migration of perhaps 200,000 Mexicans to the United States. Though most immigrants from Mexico to the United States have been looking for a more prosperous life, these early immigrants were definitely seeking security as well.

Third, the Revolution stirred up tremendous anti-Mexican feelings in the U.S. because of the actions of one revolutionary general, Francisco "Pancho" Villa. President Woodrow Wilson had at one time supported Villa in his attempts to gain power as Mexico's new leader, but had become disillusioned and dropped him. Pancho Villa was furious and retaliated by kidnapping 18 Americans from a Mexican train and murdering them in early 1916.

Then, he crossed the border with his guerrilla army and raided the town of Columbus, New Mexico on March 9, burning it and leaving 17 more Americans dead. America was outraged, and Wilson sent General John Pershing and 6,000 American soldiers into Mexico to hunt down Villa and his army. It seems odd today, but Mexico's President Carranza approved Pershing's counter-invasion, and the U.S. Army remained in Mexico for two years. They never managed to corner Pancho Villa, however. (After the revolution, in 1923, Villa too was assassinated by political enemies.[130]) But after Pancho Villa's raid in early 1916, relations with the U.S. got even more tense.

The first world war broke out in August 1914, in Europe, as Germany and the Austria-Hungarian Empire fought Britain, France, and Russia for supremacy in Europe. Britain's superior sea-power enabled it to declare a complete embargo on Germany, allowing no trade goods to enter or leave Germany by sea. By 1917, the blockade was bringing Germany to the brink of starvation, and German Foreign Secretary Arthur Zimmermann sent a secret, coded cable message to Mexico's leaders that was intercepted by the British and then handed over to the U.S. government. In translation, this astounding and outrageous document reads:

We intend to begin on the first of February unrestricted submarine warfare. We shall endeavor in spite of this to keep the United States of America neutral. In the event of this not succeeding, we make Mexico a proposal or alliance on the following basis: make war together, make peace together, generous financial support and an understanding on our part that Mexico is to reconquer the lost territory in Texas, New Mexico, and Arizona. The settlement in detail is left to you.[131]

What Zimmermann meant by "unrestricted submarine warfare" was sinking any ships carrying supplies to Britain, including ships from neutral nations like the United States. Whether unrestricted submarine attacks by themselves would have brought the U.S. into the war cannot be known, because it was the publication of the translated Zimmermann Telegraph in American newspapers that built public outrage to the breaking point and caused Congress to declare war against Germany in April 1917.

Although Mexico's then-President Venustiano Carranza did appoint a military commission to study Zimmermann's proposal when it arrived, the generals advised that Mexico was in no position to attack the United States and so Germany should be refused. Nonetheless, the American public was left with the impression that Mexico had, again, shown herself to be less than a friendly neighbor.

Enter the Ku Klux Klan

After the war ended in 1918, things became very tough in rural America, including the lands in the Southwest with significant Hispanic populations. Prices for agricultural commodities collapsed, as Europe no longer needed America to feed it. Corn, for example, dropped from the war price of $1.35 per bushel to $.61 shortly afterward.[132] Farmers had borrowed to buy land and equipment, reckoning on the high prices lasting. (Low prices for crops, bad weather, and overborrowing were early causes for the slowdown that eventually grew into the Great Depression.)

The war's end coincided with a rise in intolerance and racial violence in America. The Ku Klux Klan, a post-Civil War White vigilante group that had died out, was brought back to ugly life. The early silent movie "The Birth of a Nation" was released in 1915 and made a huge impression. At three hours running time, it was the longest and by far the most technically advanced movie to date. Probably 3 million people saw it during its first year. The movie was about the Civil War and Reconstruction, and the message was racist in the extreme. Black men were portrayed as sexually desiring of and threatening to White women. The Ku Klux Klan, shown in white robes, was depicted defending the rights of White people. Shortly after the film began its run in Atlanta, a Protestant minister led a crowd of sympathizers to Stone Mountain, Georgia, where they burned a cross.[133]

By 1920, a new Klan had spread throughout the South and Midwest, with its secret, robed members organized in cells they called "Klans." The group had newspapers, a magazine, and politicians who quite openly espoused its racist ideas. Not content just to oppress Blacks, the new Klan also railed against Roman Catholics, Jews, and foreigners. Most Hispanics in America at that time were identified as Catholic and foreign, so some units of the Klan in the Southwest turned their malignant attention to them. Klan members believed that the "races" should be separate; that Whites were biologically superior and specially favored by God; and that Catholics were something like foreign spies since the Vatican was, in their estimation, trying to control the voting of Catholics in a conspiracy. In a three-part article for the Klan's *Kourier Magazine* analyzing what it called the "Mexican problem,"[134] Hispanics were described as "lacking in character, in responsibility, overwhelmed by religion and drink." Additionally, they were portrayed as "less than human on the evolutionary scale."[135]

Texas had a large Ku Klux Klan membership during its short time of popularity. Texas Rangers, already very severe upon Mexican immigrants and those of Hispanic heritage, were by some accounts full of Klan sympathizers or even members. Besides their infamous nighttime raids and cross burnings, the Klan's biggest activities were parades. At least in South Texas, Hispanic elected officials tried to prevent these, and Laredo, Texas, was one town where authorities blocked roads, deputized armed men, and got court orders to prevent Klan parades.

In the city of Uvalde, Texas (sadly made notorious by a terrible school shooting in May 2022), a local Klan's membership list shows 355 members among the 23,000 local citizens. The city's tax collector and street supervisor were members, as were six county employees, including two county commissioners, a justice of the peace, and the sheriff.[136] The Uvalde Klan turned itself into a Saudi-style morality police, roaming the streets at night looking for Hispanics and Whites who might be out looking for an unsanctioned good time. Those found might be beaten. These activities were common among local Klans.

By 1925, fortunately, the Ku Klux Klan's influence and membership began a steep and irreversible decline. From above 2 million members at its peak, the group was down to an estimated 30,000 by 1930 as its many abuses and corruptions became publicized, and the fad faded. Unlike the very real and numerous murders of Blacks, the Klan's anti-Hispanic energy had always been tepid.[137]

Farm labor controversies lead to a political awakening

The Great Depression began at the end of the 1920s. There were many causes, but the collapse of agricultural commodity prices that followed the end of World War I was a big factor. Dry weather during the 1930s combined with destructive agricultural practices to create a "dust bowl", with low prices for commodities, failing crops, and bank takeovers of land bought on credit, creating conditions where guest workers from Mexico were no longer welcome in the United States.

The federal government began organizing the return of Mexican crop workers to their home country. According to the Library of Congress:

> As unemployment swept the U.S., hostility to immigrant workers grew, and the government began a program of repatriating immigrants to Mexico. Immigrants were offered free train rides to Mexico, and some went voluntarily, but many were either tricked or coerced into repatriation, and some U.S. citizens were deported simply on suspicion of being Mexican. All in all, hundreds of thousands of Mexican immigrants, especially farmworkers, were sent out of the country during the 1930s—many of them the same workers who had been eagerly recruited a decade before.[138]

There were, of course, permanent Hispanic residents of the U.S., and these stayed, but many others were ejected from their homes during the lengthy U.S. downturn. Yet by the end of the decade, and especially after America entered World War II as a combatant in December 1941, everything changed *again*. During the war, 16 million American men and women served in the armed forces, and myriads of others left farms to work in munitions factories, so there was a tremendous shortage of farm labor in the U.S. Again, Mexican farm workers were wanted and recruited to make up the shortfall. The government initiated the "Braceros" program in 1942, which was a series of agreements with the Mexican government to bring in contracted guest workers to help meet the American demand. This program lasted 22 years, and more than 4.5 million Mexican temporary agricultural workers were brought to the U.S. during that time.

The authorized, officially sanctioned workers were followed up by illegal workers, often called "wetbacks" in a reference to them having swum across the Rio Grande to gain illegal access to America. These illegal workers undercut Mexican temporary workers and native-born Americans, especially black and American Hispanic workers, alike. After the war, President Truman convened a presidential Commission on Migratory Labor to investigate abuses. One Black ag worker told the commission that when the illegal Mexican workers came, Americans were fired. An American Hispanic reported that the "wetbacks... don't care what the wages are... sometimes they don't get wages at all, only beans, coffee, and tortillas."[139]

After the war, American men were once again able to farm, yet the government continued the Bracero program. Although no Bracero worker was supposed to replace a domestic farm laborer, it happened, nonetheless. Also, the number of unauthorized workers continued to grow. By the early 1960s, American Hispanics began to organize to protect their agricultural field jobs from unfair foreign competition. In 1962, a young, handsome, and charismatic activist Cesar Chavez organized the United Farmworkers Union.

By 1965, the UFW began a strike against table grape growers centered in Delano, California, pulling workers from selected fields at the height of the harvest and picketing the farms, attempting to keep strikebreaking workers from crossing the lines. The growers responded by raising wages to $1.25 an hour, but this was rejected by the union as too little. Chavez called for a nationwide boycott of California non-union-picked grapes, and this caught on.[140]

Chavez became famous not just for organizing farm workers, but also for helping develop and personify a new movement for "Chicano" rights. Chicano was a derisive term for Mexican-American that Chavez and his contemporaries embraced and made into a badge of honor. The grape boycott became a protracted struggle, and during it Chavez wrote an open letter to a representative of the grape growers trying to correct the impression that his union resorted to violence to get its way. In the letter, he compared his nonviolent movement for justice to that of Martin Luther King's struggle to obtain civil rights struggle for Black Americans:

> We are men and women who have suffered and endured much, and not only because of our abject poverty but because we have been kept poor. The colors of our skins, the languages of our cultural and native origins, the lack of formal education, the exclusion from the democratic process, the numbers of our men slain in recent wars —all these burdens generation after generation have sought to demoralize us, to break our human spirit. But God knows that we are not beasts of burden, agricultural implements, or rented slaves; we are men.[141]

Cesar Chavez helped create the beginnings of a national consciousness of Hispanic Americans, different from that of the citizens of the countries Hispanics had left behind, distinctly American. And like other American low-paid laborers, his farm workers were uniquely vulnerable to cheap foreign workers newly arrived from south of the Border. To Chavez, this was unbearable.

During most of his struggle to organize farm labor, Chavez virulently opposed illegal immigrants coming into the U.S. to help break strikes. In a 1974 interview, Chavez said, "There's an awful lot of illegals coming in. . . . They're coming in by the thousands, it's just unbelievable. See, they're coming in with the consent of the immigration service."[142] He also said repeatedly, "If we can get the illegals out of California, we will win the strike overnight."[143] To gain more attention for the issue, Chavez marched to the U.S. Mexico border in 1969 to protest illegal labor coming in to take his American workers' jobs.

One thing Chavez and the United Farm Workers wanted was an end to the Bracero program. In 1964, the Republican Presidential nominee, Senator Barry Goldwater of Arizona, who had already turned off Blacks by voting against the monumental Civil Rights Act of 1964, also repelled Hispanic supporters by endorsing an extension to the Bracero program.[144] Pres. Lyndon Johnson canceled the Bracero program under pressure later that year.

In 1968, about 1,000 Hispanic high school students walked out of their Los Angeles public high school, protesting the poor quality of education there. Other walkouts quickly followed at schools and universities. A movement to offer bilingual education to non-English fluent students begins to take shape.[145]

Also in 1968, civil rights attorney Jack Greenberg founded the Mexican-American Legal Defense Fund (MALDEF) to wage legal battles to further the rights of Americans of Mexican descent. An early victory included a lawsuit that forced Texas to end at-large districts for city councils, county commissions, and school boards, because such at-large voting gave less voice to ethnic minority groups.[146] This kind of lawsuit had been sponsored previously by the NAACP and other Black civil rights groups, but MALDEF brought awareness that Hispanics were a minority that needed its rights defended as well.

Another new rights group founded the same year was (re)named the National Council of La Raza, which means "the race." A product of the Chicano movement, La Raza was a political activist organization that advocated for progressive goals like immigration amnesties and expansion, increased social welfare programs, and voter registration. Eventually, the Chicano movement faded, but MALDEF, La Raza (now named Unidos US), and several other ethnic Hispanic groups became loose parts of the left wing of the Democratic Party, responsible for keeping issues of interest to Hispanics front and center in the party.

However, the groups did give Democratic Party leaders the misleading impression that Hispanics were as progressive as were the groups trying to represent them. Democrats gained a huge advantage as these national, foundation-funded advocacy groups spent much energy in registering new Hispanic voters and steering them toward the Democratic Party. All the energy in Hispanic political organization, except for the Republican-leaning Cuban emigree community of southern Florida, was on the Democratic side.

Yet, these groups and movements were always quite liberal, and they eventually pulled Hispanic politicians into alliances with Democrats on liberal social issues like gay marriage and abortion rights. The left-leaning focus of Hispanic Democratic politicians has begun to cost the Democratic Party as the rise of Hispanic conservatives has begun to lead more Hispanics into the Republican Party.

The invention of the Hispanic ethnic label

One problem shared by government officials, academics, and advocacy groups was that there was a shortage of statistical data about people of Spanish-language heritage, since there was no unifying term to describe people who are usually referred to as Mexican-Americans, Cubans, Puerto Ricans, etc. Some readers may be surprised that it was a Republican President, Richard Nixon, who forced a change that helped unite the various people in America who came from Spanish-speaking countries into something of a coherent ethnicity. Nixon was from California. According to Leslie Sanchez, "Nixon took great interest in the Hispanic population, and he demanded that a question about Hispanic origin be included in the Census questionnaire" in 1970. It was done.[147]

The Census Bureau did this by including a new ethnic term, "HISPANIC," as one possible racial/ethnic identity people could choose when being counted. Before 1970, there were Mexican-Americans/Chicanos, Puerto Ricans, Cubans, Central Americans, etc., but there wasn't one overarching term that most people accepted. For more than 50 years, Hispanic has been the term the U.S. government uses to describe the people from two score nations who settled in this country.

Hispanic is the government's term, and probably the most accepted term used by Americans whose ancestors came from Spanish-speaking areas, but there are other terms that are used. "Latino" may be the second most popular term. Owing to the gender-specific nature of Spanish nouns, female Hispanics are sometimes referred to as "Latinas." People from New Mexico who trace their ancestry to Spain, before

Mexico got its independence, often prefer to be called "Spanish." "Chicano" is still sometimes used. More recently, left-leaning Hispanics have championed the non-gender-specific term "Latinx," yet polls have found only tiny numbers of American Hispanics prefer that term.

Having an official term (Hispanic) used by the government came in handy when the Nixon administration, always much more liberal on domestic issues than its detractors imagined, began to put the new program of affirmative action in place to give Americans from various ethnic groups a push to getting government and other jobs more in line with their percentage of the U.S. population. The basic idea behind affirmative action is that when candidates for jobs or program grants, etc., are similarly qualified, candidates coming from ethnic backgrounds considered historically disadvantaged should be given extra consideration. The concept got into trouble, however, when some universities and other more progressive institutions began turning these modest racial preferences into rigid quotas. In 1978, the Supreme Court ruled that racial quotas were unconstitutional, although it said non-quota affirmative action programs could be allowed.[148]

Although Republican officials were largely responsible for getting affirmative action going, it quickly became unpopular among many non-Hispanic White voters and Republican Party officials. Gallup found in 2018 that 66% of Hispanic adults favored affirmative action programs that help ethnic minorities.[149] Perhaps the loud GOP opposition to affirmative action is one of the reasons so many Hispanics have had for gravitating toward the Democratic Party over the past few decades. But as we are seeing, things may be changing.

Chapter Eight

Why It's Simply Wrong To Suggest Hispanics' Experience In America Is The Same As That Of Black Americans

J esse Jackson's political star peaked so long ago that today it's hard to remember just how electric a figure he was in Democratic Party politics in the 1970s and '80s.

Jackson first rose to prominence as a young aide to the Rev. Martin Luther King, Jr. With other advisors, he was nearby when King was shot down by a racist assassin at a Memphis hotel in 1968 and spoke movingly about the experience on national TV. In the late 1970s, Jackson, himself a minister like MLK, formed Operation PUSH (People United to Save Humanity) and spoke passionately to largely Black audiences about the need to accept personal responsibility in order to be able to take advantage of the new opportunities civil rights had made available.

When Jackson decided to make a serious run for the 1984 Democratic Presidential nomination, he became a household name. He ran hard but found it difficult to gain a broad audience beyond his Black voter base. He didn't win the nomination but made an unforgettable speech. On August 18, 1984, Jackson spoke at the Democratic Convention, explaining what he had been trying to accomplish in his campaign. The moment was riveting. He proposed a "rainbow coalition" that would allow liberal policies to gain majority status.

"We must forgive each other, redeem each other, regroup, and move on," he said. "Our flag is red, white and blue, but our nation is a rainbow—red, yellow, brown, black and white—and we're all precious in God's sight." The speech continued, "If Blacks vote in great numbers, progressive Whites win. It's the only way progressive Whites win. If Blacks vote in great numbers, Hispanics win. When Blacks, Hispanics, and progressive Whites vote, women win. When women win, children win. When women and children win, workers win. We must all come up together."[150]

The Rainbow Coalition speech was given 38 years ago, but it remains a powerful idea, almost a controlling paradigm, for Democratic progressives. Blacks, Hispanics, Asians, women and LGBTQs are now routinely urged to make common cause to promote their mutually held liberal policy views and gain actual political power. In a way, this is the idea Judis and Teixeira advanced with *The Emerging Democratic Majority* in 2002.

Indeed, Hispanics, Blacks, and Asians are often referred to as "people of color" by followers of this idea. But a rainbow coalition of Hispanics and Blacks does seem to presuppose that these two groups are in many ways parallel, that they pair well together, and that their world views have been forged from suffering similar struggles in this nation. In this view, both groups have had to overcome White supremacy and other forms of structural racism. In a 2015 blog, one political writer made a typical statement, "Over the past few months, America has seen the images of young, black Americans protesting for better treatment by the police and, more acutely, protesting against generations of unequal treatment in our society. Latinos share many of the same experiences of exclusion, disadvantage, and barriers to opportunity."[151]

Voting patterns from the past few decades might tend to confirm for casual students that Hispanics and Blacks see their fortunes linked somewhat together and certainly to the Democratic Party. In the 2012 Presidential election, for example, Hispanics gave 71% of their votes to Democrat Barack Obama, and Blacks gave him 93% of theirs.[152] Obviously, large majorities of both groups supported Pres. Obama, but did that mean they did so out of solidarity with each other? Does it make sense to lump these two gigantic ethnic groups together?

I tend to think not. The journey and experience of Black people in America and the experience of Hispanics here could not be more different in most respects. In this chapter, I will lay out how different their stories are.

How Blacks and Hispanics got to America

Most Black Americans, except for fairly recent immigrants from Africa or the Caribbean Islands, are descendants of U.S. slavery. African slaves were first brought to this country in the year 1619, a year before the Pilgrims landed on Plymouth Rock in Massachusetts. One of the defining characteristics of European settlement in America has been a near-perennial labor shortage. America had vast land that could be farmed, but during our first two centuries, never enough farmers. Using reasoning that seems both abhorrent and bizarre to us today, English colonial settlers decided to make up for their short numbers by importing kidnapped laborers from Africa.

These enslaved individuals were considered property, with no hope of freedom for themselves or their offspring *EVER!* They could be beaten like animals with no recourse to the law. They could be worked literally to death. They could be rented out, they could be sexually attacked by White masters. As bad as all this was, after a brief but bloody slave rebellion in Virginia in 1831 in which 55 Whites were murdered, slave states panicked and passed new and even more oppressive laws.[153] After this, in many slave states, it became illegal to free slaves or allow them to purchase their own freedom. It was also illegal to teach them to read or to allow them to congregate. Naturally, they were not allowed to own property or vote. Their marriages were not recognized by the law. Slave families could be and were regularly split up and sold apart.

Moreover, this was not a fate suffered by a small number of people and thus lost to history. By the time of the Civil War, White people owned 3,953,760 Black slaves in this country.[154] Fortunately, before the Southern state laws had made it impossible, many slaves had obtained their freedom one way or the other, and about 500,000 free Blacks also lived in the U.S. by the beginning of the war.[155]

Contrast all this with the experience of Hispanics here. None were slaves, unless perhaps they were also of African descent. As stated earlier, there were not many Hispanics yet living in America's Southwest and West when the United States took control, but those who did were made U.S. citizens by treaty with Mexico. Hispanics could and did own property, and had the right to vote, to marry, to inherit, to enter the professions, and to become educated. Some opportunities were more limited to Hispanics as a generally poorer and foreign-seeming group, but the discrimination was episodic and spotty rather than constant and general. Having said that, Anglos were interested in maintaining dominance and put many roadblocks in the way when the number of Hispanics began rising.

Blacks were united by a shared story; Hispanics were not

When Africans were pulled away from their homes and sold into slavery in North America, they lost everything but themselves. They lost their native languages, since they had previously spoken a plethora of African dialects, and, once in America, they could not even understand each other. (Over time, being forced to be solely English speakers became an advantage for Black Americans, compared to Hispanics, since they had no language barrier to overcome.) They lost their history, and it's a rare descendant of African slaves who knows much or even anything about where their ancestors were taken from. They lost their original beliefs. It's one thing to convert voluntarily to a new faith. It's quite another thing to have your old faith erased.

Black Americans lost much, but they gained some shared experiences as well. They shared a uniting story of misery and mistreatment at the hands of White Americans. Eventually, most of them shared a religion with their captors. It was a religion whose very tenets undermined the legitimacy of owning human beings and whose best storylines involved reaching freedom from slavery of both the literal and moral varieties. Since Black Americans had no collective memory of "the old country," their former ethnic identities did not divide them as it did for most immigrant groups, including Hispanics. When some government officials and many civic leaders, both White and Black, promoted opportunities to move back to Africa, few former slaves or descendants of slaves were interested.

Unlike Black descendants of American slavery, Hispanics know well which of more than a score of origin nations and islands, all with distinct histories, is their own. And Hispanics differ because they or their ancestors came of their own volition. Some came from desperate poverty or escaped from war, others were fairly prosperous in their countries of origin and moved to the United States to become more so. Some were well educated upon arrival, though many more did not enjoy the lavishly financed free education that is the birthright of American children.

Black Americans are known as a racial group, and three-quarters of them see their race as a primary part of their identity.[156] Hispanic Americans, on the other hand, don't see themselves as a racial group since they consider themselves as American Indian, Black, mixed race, and increasingly, White.

Hispanics frequently refer to themselves by their countries of origin. They call themselves Cubans, Salvadorans, Bolivians, Venezuelans, Dominicans, etc., rather than Hispanic, Latino, or other terms that speak more of ethnicity than geography. Thus, their ethnic backgrounds sometimes divide rather than unite them.[157]

Persecution and the lack of persecution

After the Civil War, the U.S. quickly added three amendments to the Constitution to address the special situation of Black Americans. The 13th amendment made slavery illegal everywhere. The 14th stated that persons born in the U.S. and who were "subject to the jurisdiction therein" were to be considered citizens of the United States—this was to make clear that ex-slaves and their offspring were citizens. Also, the 14th amendment stated that the government could not limit their rights, "nor shall any State deprive any person of life, liberty, or property, without due process of law; nor deny to any person within its jurisdiction the equal protection of the laws." Finally, the 15th amendment declared that "The right of citizens of the United States to vote shall not be denied or abridged by the United States or by any State on account of race, color, or previous condition of servitude."

As long as Union troops occupied the former Confederate states, Blacks enjoyed a good deal of freedom. More than 90% of Black men registered to vote, and Blacks were elected to Congress. Yet almost as soon as the troops were withdrawn, Southern legislatures passed laws making it difficult to impossible for Blacks to vote. By 1940, only three percent of Blacks were registered to vote in the South.[158] Segregation was universal. Education provided to Black children was grossly underfunded and inferior. Blacks murdered by Whites were almost never prosecuted. Economic advancement was extremely difficult.

Hispanics faced a very different America after the Civil War. Although White local governments occasionally used English literacy tests or other devices to tamp down Hispanic voting, in general their modest numbers and light-colored skin made them seem less of a threat to dominant White society. Election records show Hispanic Americans voting throughout the post-war period. For example, California Republican Romualdo Pacheco became the 12th Governor of California in 1875 after serving in other statewide elected offices. He was later elected to Congress.[159] As citizens from the time of the Mexican-American War, Hispanic Americans held offices large and small throughout the Southwest, as they did in Florida and other acquired territories. For example, Joseph Marion Hernández, a plantation owner and soldier, represented Florida in Congress as a territorial delegate from 1821 to 1822.[160]

As to social status enforced by laws, the status of Blacks and Hispanics couldn't have been more different. After the Civil War, laws were passed throughout the United States, including in many Northern and Western states, forbidding marriage between Whites and Blacks, or in some cases between Whites and Native Americans or Asians. None of these laws covered Hispanics, who were always free from a legal point of view to marry within the White community. As stated earlier, Hispanics were generally considered to be "White" in terms of their race.

Civil Rights struggle versus the fight to organize politically

Having suffered collectively for hundreds of years in this country, Black Americans naturally are drawn together through this common history of suffering. Beginning early in the 20th century and accelerating by the 1940s, Blacks organized together in a movement to demand the civil rights the Constitution, as amended after the war, had promised them. The Civil Rights movement eventually involved hundreds of thousands of Blacks marching, petitioning, boycotting, and otherwise working together to receive full rights.

An early victory for the movement was when the Supreme Court in the 1954 Brown Versus the Board of Education case struck down as unconstitutional the "separate but equal" education doctrine that had been used to justify segregated schools. There was the fabled March on Washington in 1963 by hundreds of thousands of Blacks (and sympathetic Whites), capped off by Martin Luther King's titanic "I have a dream" speech. The next year, Congress passed the Civil Rights Act of 1964 which outlawed discrimination "on the basis of race, color, religion, sex or national origin." The law made discrimination in hiring an illegal act, for example, and forbade discrimination in housing, education, and many other areas of life. The 1965 Voting Rights Act made southern state practices such as poll taxes that prevented Blacks from voting, illegal. This opened the way for Blacks to vote in large numbers and hold elected office everywhere. In a symbolic victory, Atlanta elected its first black mayor, Maynard Jackson, in October 1973.[161]

The struggle to win full rights as American citizens in the middle half of the 20th century was yet another thing that brought Black Americans together, gave them a common story and a joint victory, and knitted them in social and political cohesion unlike any other major ethnic group. Franklin Roosevelt (and especially his wife Eleanor) triggered the mass movement of Black voters from the Republican Party which had been their home since Abraham Lincoln's emancipation. FDR's poverty-fighting efforts during the Great Depression of the 1930s sparked the imagination and inspired hope in Black Americans as they began voting heavily for Democrats. Despite the Democratic Party's very long history of supporting slavery, Jim Crow laws, and legalized oppression, the party increasingly changed its image to one of a deliverer of civil rights as the 20th century wore on, and in the last presidential election, in 2020, Joe Biden received the nod from 92% of all Black voters.[162] This united Black vote for Democrats now – as for Republicans before FDR – comes from hundreds of years of common struggle.

As in the other categories in this chapter, Hispanics have no parallel experience with the Civil Rights struggle. Being usually considered White for legal purposes in American history, Hispanics did not need a Civil Rights Act to win legal equality. The discrimination many of them faced, though very real, was not usually reinforced by laws. Employers generally have not needed to be compelled by laws to hire Hispanics. White employers have rushed to hire Hispanics and have often agitated in Congress to increase immigration so they could hire more.

There were ugly exceptions to this, however. In California, beginning in the 1920s, large numbers of Hispanic workers began coming to California to pick crops and otherwise work on farms. Though the state did not pass discriminatory laws, towns often took it upon themselves to take actions such as to segregate swimming pools or manipulate school district lines to keep Hispanics separated, often arguing that separate schools helped the Mexican-American kids catch up.[163] By 1946, however, a federal judge ruled this kind of school segregation illegal. Spontaneous bias from private citizens, such as the signs hung in some restaurants saying "No dogs or Mexicans" were harder to eliminate and of course left a psychic scar.

Most Hispanics here today did not suffer

Some readers will disagree, but it seems to me that by the time most Hispanics immigrated to this country (after 1965), America had put behind it most of the real barriers to progress and participation faced by earlier generations of Hispanics. As a matter of fact, most Hispanics in America can trace their immigrant roots to 40 or 50 years ago or less. They just weren't here for the bad old days of racial segregation, and as I've shown, Hispanics even in those earlier days faced only sporadic oppression.

One proof of this is how incredibly optimistic most Hispanics are about living in this country. Rasmussen Reports, in the special poll of American Hispanics undertaken for this book, found the overwhelming majority believe that America is "open and welcoming" to "Hispanics like you."

There is some evidence that Hispanics are tiring of being lumped in with other minority voters by Democratic Party leaders. David Brooks put it this way. "'People of color' is not a thing. It was always odd to create a group identity that covered a vast majority of humanity.

In this country the phrase 'people of color' sometimes papers over a wide array of different ethnic experiences. It contributes to a simplistic oppressor/oppressed narrative in which white Republicans are supposed to be on one side and P.O.C. are supposed to be on the other." Brooks summed it up, "That made it harder to anticipate that Trump would make the impressive gains among Hispanics in 2020 that he did."[164]

Chapter Nine

What Hispanics *REALLY* Think about Immigration

Mostly, when political analysts try to interpret what this or that group is thinking, they have to work with sketchy direct evidence. It's like reading tea leaves. You do the best you can. Realistically, how can you tell what millions of voters are thinking? This is not a book about the science of polling. However, since special polls were commissioned just for this book, and because I quote liberally from many, many polls in making my various points throughout the book, I will take just a few paragraphs to discuss how polling works and why it's a bit more reliable than many people assume.

In modern times, one of the favorite tools of analysts has been public opinion polling. George Gallup essentially invented modern polling in the 1930s. An early proof of polling accuracy happened in 1936, when the Gallup Poll correctly predicted that Pres. Franklin Roosevelt would win a second term.[165] Now, of course, today there are dozens of polling organizations. Though their methods differ in many respects, the basic idea is the same with all of them. The key idea is that if you randomly select perhaps as few as 800 people to represent a much bigger group, such as all U.S. voters, the laws of averages and randomness work together so that those 800 will answer questions very close to the answers you would get if you asked the entire voting population. To some ears, this notion sounds unlikely, even impossible. How can 800 give the same answers the entire 180 million would?

The Harvard Business Review looked at this question in a 2016 article. "It may seem strange to assert that a poll can measure the preferences of an entire country by talking to as few as 800 people, but the math works if those 800 people are selected through a truly random process," the article stated. "Think about it this way: a certain proportion of Americans currently intend to vote for Donald Trump in the upcoming Presidential election: we can't directly observe it, but we know it's there. Polling is how we indirectly estimate that proportion. Over the course of the poll, you might, by pure chance, call a cluster of people who all intend to vote for Trump, but so long as the sample is random, they'll be averaged out by those who don't intend to do so, and, as the sample gets bigger, the average of the sample gets closer and closer to the true proportion. The problem comes if the sample isn't really random."[166]

The huge catch is that you can't ask *truly* random respondents: You have to find people willing and able to answer your questions. So you must try hard to make sure that those you do ask are representative of the whole. For instance, if you simply call people on their home phones in the middle of the day, you're likely to get too many people who don't go to work, such as retirees. The closer the sample group resembles the entire population, the more accurate your poll will be. Obviously, getting this right takes a pile of experience, technical know-how, plus highly tuned instincts. Accurate polling is both art and science.

How accurate are political polls today?

The reputation of political polling has taken lots of hits in recent elections for a number of reasons. First, as unsolicited phone sales calls have mushroomed in number, many people no longer answer the phone if they do not recognize the number or if the number is not clearly labeled by caller id. I am one of those people. If the call doesn't come up as someone I know or labeled as a business I want to hear from, I let it go to voicemail. Today, many people assume that since "normal" people like themselves don't take polling calls, therefore political polls cannot reflect the views of "normal" voters.

Whereas this thought does have some merit, the logic falls apart upon closer inspection. In fact, I think this charge arises from a logical fallacy. Let's agree for argument's sake that 90% of America's phone users do not answer unknown calls anymore. If so, that means there are still 10% of phone users that do answer most calls. Here's the question: are the political views of the 10% different from that of the 90%? Or is the one thing the 90% have in common: they don't like talking to salespeople? I think it is the latter.

To reduce dependence on people answering phone calls, many pollsters are now supplementing or replacing phone calls by administering their surveys to online groups of respondents who have agreed to take surveys.

A second standard criticism of polling is that many political polls, while getting the winners right, have been missing the margin of victories by much larger margins than in the past. Fortunately, the accuracy or inaccuracy of political polling has been studied a lot. The *FiveThirtyEight* blog, named that because there are 538 electoral college votes in presidential elections, specializes in reporting on and rating political polls using objective measures. One measure is whether the poll accurately predicted the outcome of the election. Election polls are different from many other kinds of polls because actual voting results in the end show which polls were correct. Did the person they said would win in fact win? A second measure for rating polls is by how many points they were off in predicting the margin of victory.

In *FiveThirtyEight's* huge ongoing study of all reputable polling companies, all the election public polls of each company are examined years back. After looking at a huge number of election polls for the 2020 election cycle, *Fivethirtyeight* found a wide range in accuracy (or inaccuracy) about the margin of victories. But on the criteria of predicting the outcome of elections, it found that the polls on average were about as accurate as usual. In 2020, 80% of the presidential general election polls that were taken within 21 days of the election got the winner right. Over the past 24 years of polling that *Fivethirtyeight* studied, the average correct outcome percentage was also exactly 80%. So, the four out of every five polls taken just before an election in 2020 that got the winner right was neither better nor worse than in the recent past.[167]

Our polling with Rasmussen Reports

All this is to say that not all polls are born equal. At NumbersUSA, we have used Rasmussen Reports to do much of our polling for a number of years now. The *FiveThirtyEight* study I've mentioned found that Rasmussen's surveys in the 2020 election cycle were within 2.8 points ("average error") of the final outcome. That's the third best accuracy of the 25 polling firms rated in the study. Rasmussen's "statistical bias," which calculates whether there is a bias toward one party or the other, was just 1 point, which tied for second best of all 25 firms.

Beginning in December 2019, we've sponsored Rasmussen's every-other-week Immigration Index. As they describe this tool, "The Index is based on a series of questions designed to determine whether voters are moving toward an immigration system that encourages more immigration to the United States or one that reduces the level of immigration here." There are 10 questions asked of likely voters (all Rasmussen Reports survey-takers are screened to see if they regularly vote). The very first question will give you the flavor of the Index questions: "On the question of illegal immigration, is the government doing too much or too little to reduce illegal border crossings and vis-itor overstays? Or is the level of action about right?" The 10 questions are not changed; they are asked by Rasmussen almost nightly, month after month, year after year.

The very first time the questions were asked, the answers given by those first 1,250 survey takers were tabulated and given a score of 100. How this index works is that no individual question is lifted out as more important than any other. Rather, it's how *this* week's survey takers answered the questions compared to *last* week's and all other weeks. For polling the week of Independence Day 2020, for example, the Immigration Index stood at 87.7. This meant that the answers given by voters in that recent poll were about 12 percent more favorable toward generally *lower* levels of immigration than the answers from the original survey takers in December of 2019. In fact, the Index score has been lower than 100 every week Joe Biden has been President.

Each time the Index is updated, which is every two weeks, another 1,250 likely voters are surveyed. This is more than enough for reliable results for the overall American electorate, but only 160 Hispanics are polled each time (matching their portion of the overall electorate). Yet over an entire year, several thousand Hispanic likely voters are asked the same 10 standardized questions about various aspects of immigration policy.

Grouping all the Hispanic responses Rasmussen got over an entire year has created sufficient size to provide us with a wealth of reliable information about the attitudes of many subgroups of Hispanic voters by age, education, politics, ideology, religion, residence, family, income and more. This leads me to discuss a basic problem that polling firms have in accurately measuring public opinion of ethnic minority groups such as Asians, Blacks, and Hispanics. As discussed earlier, it's possible to get a fairly accurate reading of public opinion using as few as 800 people if you are sufficiently skilled in designing how many people you will need in key categories to approximate the U.S. population. For a political poll, for example, most pollsters make sure they interview enough men and women; people of various age groups; and appropriate numbers of Republicans, Democrats, and Independents. The most careful polling firms publish exactly how many people they managed to reach from these respective groups.

The problem is that whereas polls of 800 or 1,000 or even 1,500 Americans might give you an excellent, largely accurate view of the electorate's views of various questions ("Which candidate will you vote for?"), it isn't nearly enough to accurately find the views of *subgroups* such as Hispanics. Let's take a real-world example, Mark Penn's Harvard-CAPS Harris Poll, one of the polling outfits I respect the very most. The Harvard-CAPS Harris Poll in May 2022 interviewed 1,963 registered voters, an unusually large number compared to many polls. Because of the great care Penn takes asking his questions, and because of the large sample size he uses, the Harvard-CAPS Harris polls results are always taken very seriously by me.

In May's example, although nearly 2,000 registered voters were sampled, only 139 Hispanics were reached. The poll's assumption, according to the crosstabs document released with the poll, was that 13% of those interviewed should be Hispanic, to match the percentage of Hispanic registered voters in the U.S. population. But as many firms have found, it is more difficult finding ethnic minority representatives to give your poll to than finding non-Hispanic White voters. So, in order to fulfill their "weighting" requirement of 13% Hispanics, the poll gives extra "weight" to the 139 they did interview in order to get them up to the 250 they had been seeking to interview; 250 would be 13% of the 2,000 interviewed, in keeping with the Hispanic share of registered voters.[168] But in the end, they're trying to figure out what Hispanic voters think on various topics based on a big handful of individuals. Too small for accuracy. In truth, having just 139 people represent a population of over 18 million registered Hispanic voters[169] is not as impossible as it sounds, but talking to such a small number does make your results lots less accurate. Using the standard formula for calculating the margin of error, surveying a group of 139 randomly selected people to represent a total population of 18 million should yield the same answers 95% of the time with an 8.3% margin of error.[170]

The 8.3% margin of error is a pretty big margin. If 55% of the Hispanics surveyed were to say that they intend to vote for a Democrat for Congress this November, with an 8.5% margin of error, that response may be dead on if you asked another 139 Hispanics the same questions *OR* it could be 8.5% different. So, the real answer could be that 55% of all Hispanic voters plan at this time to vote for a Democrat this fall, OR that only 46.5% plan to vote Democratic, OR that 63.5% might be planning to do so. Literally, if you poll 139 Hispanic randomly selected registered voters 100 times (different people each time), your answer to any one question can be expected to vary by 8.5% with such a small sample size.

That's why I was delighted when it occurred to us that even though the Rasmussen Immigration Index questions were asked of only about 150 Hispanic likely voters each time the poll was run, it was run 26 times a year. Therefore, by looking at how Hispanic voters answered the immigration policy questions over the entire year of 2021, our sample size is not 150, but rather 3,503. This gets our margin of error down to only 1.8%, a splendidly tiny number. Rasmussen didn't just poll Hispanic voters, however. In the course of 2021, 26,251 White likely voters were polled, as well as 3,301 Black likely voters. The truly great thing about having such a big sample size is that some of the subgroups within the sample, such as working class Hispanics versus college-educated Hispanics, *also* have a very respectable margin of error. We get accuracy up and down the entire poll.

Of course, taking answers given over an entire year's time and stitching them together as a single "virtual" poll does have one limitation. By its nature, it can only be seen as the *average* of Hispanic opinion on immigration policy from the year 2021. If Hispanic likely voters moved more toward tighter or looser immigration policies during the year, this survey would not be able to track that, only their average views throughout the year. Noting that one limitation, however, here is the data.

The REAL immigration views of Hispanic voters

So, with all that out of the way, what do Hispanic Likely Voters in the U.S. think U.S. immigration policy should be? You're about to find out, and I feel sure some of the answers will surprise you. As just noted, these results come from polling by Rasmussen Reports, which was rated in the top three of 25 polling firms for accuracy in the 2020 elections. The results for all the subgroups of Hispanics have a high degree of reliability because of the massive size of the survey.

In all the following tables of poll results, I have highlighted with black boxes and white type answers I think are worth special notice.

Poll Question 1: "On the question of illegal immigration, is the government doing too much or too little to reduce illegal border crossings and visitor overstays?"

	Too much	Too little	About right	Not sure
All Hispanics	21%	53%	19%	7%
Gender				
Men	20%	56%	21%	4%
Women	22%	52%	18%	9%
Age				
18–39	28%	43%	21%	8%
40–64	13%	66%	16%	5%
65+	11%	62%	20%	8%
Party				
Democrat	25%	42%	25%	8%
Republican	20%	63%	14%	3%
Independent/Other	15%	62%	14%	8%

	Too much	Too little	About right	Not sure
Ideology				
Conservative	22%	61%	13%	3%
Moderate	17%	54%	20%	8%
Liberal	24%	42%	28%	7%
Religion				
Evangelical Christian	23%	56%	16%	5%
Protestant	17%	63%	16%	4%
Catholic	19%	51%	23%	7%
Other or none	23%	50%	18%	9%
Education Level				
No college degree	25%	**49%**	18%	9%
Graduated college	18%	57%	20%	6%
Income				
Under $100,000	21%	53%	19%	6%
Over $100,000	21%	52%	21%	6%

Rasmussen Reports, 2021. 3,503 likely Hispanic voters. Margin of error, 1.8%.

The first question asks if survey takers felt the government was doing enough to stop illegal immigration at the U.S.-Mexico border. As the chart shows, only 21% said "Too much." The biggest group, 53%, said the government isn't doing enough to stop illegal immigration. And 19% felt that the government is doing about the right amount to stop it. This is an interesting finding, meaning only about a fifth of Hispanic voters believed the government was enforcing the border too vigorously during Pres. Biden's first year.

A majority took the opposite view—*not enough* was being done to stop illegal immigration. As for many of the questions in the Rasmussen Immigration Index polling, non-Hispanic Whites took a somewhat harder line, with 59% of Whites saying there was "Too little" enforcement, while 46% (a plurality) of Black likely voters felt that way. *(Neither of these groups is shown in the tabular data.)* Back to Hispanics, the Rasmussen polling had a robust group of subgroups identified, including gender, various age ranges, political party affiliation, education level, income level, religion, city/suburb/small town/rural. By robust, I mean that there were many people from every category.

For example, the religious identity of those Hispanics surveyed in 2021. There were 671 Evangelicals, 415 Other Protestants, 1,212

Catholics, 130 Jews, 154 Muslims, 166 Atheists, and 530 "Other." For the Evangelicals, for example, the margin of error is just 4%, very low for a polling subgroup. For Catholics, it is less than 3%. For space purposes, I'm compressing some groups, like religion, into fewer categories. The Poll Question 1 table shows the topline number, plus it shows how various subgroups answered the question.

As for one example of what more the government might do, a later poll by IPSOS, Axios and Telemundo found a majority of Hispanics support continuing Pres. Trump's Title 42, which made it temporarily easier to expel illegal aliens soon after they cross the border during the pandemic. That poll was not limited to likely voters, but did find higher support for continuing Title 42 among 2nd- and 3rd-generation Hispanics.[171]

Poll Question 2: "In trying to control illegal immigration, should the government mandate that all employers use the federal electronic E-Verify system to help ensure that they hire only legal workers for U.S. jobs?"

	Yes	No	Not sure
All Hispanics	67%	22%	12%
Gender			
Men	73%	18%	9%
Women	63%	24%	13%
Age			
18–39	60%	28%	11%
40–64	75%	15%	11%
65+	70%	14%	16%
Party			
Democrat	60%	28%	12%
Republican	79%	12%	8%
Independent/Other	67%	19%	14%
Ideology			
Conservative	79%	14%	7%
Moderate	64%	22%	14%
Liberal	55%	33%	12%
Religion			
Evangelical Christian	76%	16%	8%
Protestant	72%	18%	9%

	Yes	No	Not sure
Catholic	65%	24%	11%
Other or none	61%	24%	15%
Education Level			
No college degree	62%	25%	13%
Graduated college	71%	19%	10%
Income			
Under $100,000	66%	23%	12%
Over $100,000	73%	19%	8%

Rasmussen Reports, 2021. 3,503 likely Hispanic voters. Margin of error, 1.8%.

The second question in Rasmussen Research's Immigration Index is about the federal government's E-Verify system. E-Verify was created by Congress in 1996 as a way for employers who have just hired a new employee to check if that employee is actually authorized to work in the United States. Illegal immigrants, of course, are not authorized to work here. Despite many recommendations for a quarter of a century to mandate E-Verify for all employers, Congress has always chosen to keep the system voluntary. The system works on a pretty simple premise. To get a job with an employer using E-Verify, new hires have to provide a Social Security number, which all employers have to have for tax purposes, anyway. (In some very narrow cases, other documentation can be presented, if you are a foreign student with a work permit, for example.)

E-Verify verifies work authorization by comparing employee information taken from an I-9 form (the paper-based employee eligibility verification form used for all new hires) against existing Social Security Administration and DHS databases. E-Verify itself is not a database and creates no new databases. The only time E-Verify pings anything other than the existing social security database is when the new hire has provided immigration documents AND there is no match of name, birthdate, and SSN in the social security database. Then, and only then, the system pings a DHS database on aliens.

If the information matches, that employee is confirmed as eligible to work in the United States. If there's a mismatch, E-Verify will alert the employer, and the employee will be allowed to work while he or she resolves the problem. It is much better to know there is a problem with your social security information than to find that out later when you retire and have trouble getting social security payments.

The Obama administration made the use of E-Verify mandatory for all federal contractors. Since most really large companies do business with the government, and since many other companies voluntarily use the E-Verify system to assure themselves they are using legal employees, about half of all new hires in America in recent years have had their Social Security information authenticated using E-Verify. Because the system has a deserved reputation for accuracy, ease-of-use and virtually no cost, it is very popular with both the public and the employers that use it. People love the idea that they don't have to compete with illegal aliens who are using fake or stolen Social Security cards to illegally get jobs. Unfortunately, businesses that don't have contracts with the federal government and don't mind hiring illegal workers, or that deliberately seek them out, are currently not required to use E-Verify in most states.

There are an estimated 12 million or more illegal aliens living in the U.S. today, and most of them have on-the-books jobs with firms that do not use E-Verify. Those firms have no way of verifying whether the Social Security numbers presented by the new hires are authentic or stolen. If they look real, the companies have to accept them if they don't E-Verify. More than one million illegal immigrants are estimated to use fake cards that utilize Social Security numbers of actual legal workers; in other words, document fraud on a massive scale.[172] I wondered how Hispanic likely voters, who of course are all U.S. citizens, would feel about forcing every single employer in the U.S. to use the E-Verify system to "ensure that [companies] hire only legal workers for U.S. jobs?"

The answer was dramatic: 68% of Hispanic voters think that using the E-Verify system should be *mandatory*. Only 22% disagree. That's a three-to-one margin—extremely high. Hispanic men felt even stronger about it, with 73% of them feeling E-Verify use should be mandatory, and only 18% disagreeing. It's not surprising that Republican Hispanics backed mandatory E-Verify by 79% to 12%, but even Democrats were in favor, 60% to 28%. Self-described liberals actually favored E-Verify by 55% to 33%.

I have often heard sensitive people suggest that E-Verify might be a bad idea because they assumed it would somehow be offensive to Hispanics. Ever since NumbersUSA has been polling this question, however, I've been able to reassure people on that score. "You don't understand how Hispanics feel about illegal workers," I inform them. "The vast majority of Hispanics in America are citizens," I say. "They don't want to compete with illegal aliens any more than you do." As you see in Poll Question 2 above, the evidence on that matter could not be clearer.

Poll Question 3: "Do you strongly favor, somewhat favor, somewhat oppose or strongly oppose giving lifetime work permits to most of the approximately two million illegal residents who came to this country when they were minors?"

	Strongly Favor	Somewhat Favor	Somewhat Oppose	Strongly Oppose	Not Sure
All Hispanics	32%	26%	15%	22%	5%
Gender					
Men	31%	26%	15%	24%	4%
Women	32%	26%	15%	21%	6%
Age					
18-39	35%	32%	13%	13%	7%
40-64	27%	20%	17%	33%	2%
65+	32%	19%	15%	29%	6%
Party					
Democrat	43%	37%	11%	15%	5%
Republican	24%	25%	17%	30%	4%
Independent/Other	22%	26%	20%	27%	6%
Ideology					
Conservative	27%	28%	15%	27%	3%
Moderate	27%	27%	18%	21%	6%
Liberal	41%	21%	10%	19%	4%
Religion					
Evangelical Christian	28%	26%	15%	27%	3%
Protestant	28%	26%	19%	24%	4%
Catholic	33%	29%	14%	20%	5%
Other or none	35%	24%	14%	14%	21%

	Strongly Favor	Somewhat Favor	Somewhat Oppose	Strongly Oppose	Not Sure
Education Level					
No college degree	33%	30%	15%	17%	6%
Graduated college	31%	23%	15%	27%	4%
Income					
Under $100,000	32%	26%	14%	22%	5%
Over $100,000	32%	26%	16%	23%	3%

Rasmussen Reports, 2021. 3,503 likely Hispanic voters. Margin of error, 1.8%.

If the right deal could be struck, most members of Congress would probably grant an amnesty to so-called Dreamers who came illegally to the United States when they were minors. For my organization, the right deal would include obvious things like stopping most future illegal immigration by including mandatory E-Verify and an end to chain migration so amnesty recipients could not create endless flows of additional foreign workers into the country. As suggested by the answers to Poll Question 3 and the ones in the survey on E-Verify and chain migration, most Hispanic voters would likely prefer the same criteria. But backers of a DREAM amnesty have never wanted their amnesty enough to cut a deal to get it.

Poll Question 4: "Do you strongly favor, somewhat favor, somewhat oppose or strongly oppose giving lifetime work permits to most of the estimated 12 million illegal residents of all ages who currently reside in the United States?"

	Strongly Favor	Somewhat Favor	Somewhat Oppose	Strongly Oppose	Not Sure
All Hispanics	24%	22%	16%	33%	5%
Gender					
Men	24%	22%	15%	36%	3%
Women	25%	23%	16%	30%	6%

	Strongly Favor	Somewhat Favor	Somewhat Oppose	Strongly Oppose	Not Sure
Age					
18–39	31%	29%	16%	19%	6%
40–64	17%	15%	15%	49%	4%
65+	**20%**	**17%**	14%	**45%**	4%
Party					
Democrat	34%	28%	13%	20%	5%
Republican	19%	16%	**16%**	**45%**	3%
Independent/Other	13%	20%	**20%**	**41%**	6%
Ideology					
Conservative	23%	21%	15%	39%	2%
Moderate	18%	23%	19%	33%	6%
Liberal	37%	23%	11%	25%	5%
Religion					
Evangelical Christian	24%	20%	15%	39%	3%
Protestant	16%	20%	20%	40%	4%
Catholic	26%	25%	14%	29%	5%
Other or none	26%	22%	16%	30%	6%
Education Level					
No college degree	14%	28%	18%	25%	5%
Graduated college	25%	18%	13%	38%	5%
Income					
Under $100,000	24%	24%	16%	30%	5%
Over $100,000	27%	19%	14%	38%	3%

Rasmussen Reports, 2021. 3,503 likely Hispanic voters. Margin of error, 1.8%.

Hispanics are deeply divided about whether they favor "giving lifetime work permits to most of the estimated 12 million illegal residents of all ages who currently reside in the United States."

While 46% of Hispanics support amnestying most of the 12 million, 49% oppose this move (with 33% who "strongly oppose" it). There is a lot of difference among age groups. Taking just the 50–64 year-olds *(not shown separately in the table)*, only 26% support the 12 million-person amnesty, and 71% oppose it, with 55% of them "strongly" opposing. Another group that overwhelmingly opposes the amnesty is political independents, who belong to no political party. While 33% of them support an amnesty, fully 61% are against it (almost identical to Republicans who oppose it by 61%-to-35%).

Poll Question 5: "Recent federal policies have added about one million new permanent immigrants to the United States each year. Which is closest to the number of new immigrants the government should be adding each year—fewer than 500,000, 750,000, one million, one and a half million, or more than one and a half million?"

	Fewer Than 500,000	750,000	1,000,000	1,500,000	More Than 1,500,000	Not Sure
All Hispanics	38%	20%	18%	7%	8%	10%
Gender						
Men	38%	21%	20%	7%	8%	7%
Women	38%	19%	17%	7%	8%	11%
Age						
18–39	28%	24%	20%	9%	8%	10%
40–64	49%	15%	15%	5%	7%	8%
65+	48%	15%	15%	5%	7%	10%
Party						
Democrat	30%	21%	20%	8%	10%	11%
Republican	48%	18%	15%	7%	5%	7%
Independent/Other	42%	19%	17%	7%	6%	10%
Ideology						
Conservative	46%	22%	17%	6%	4%	6%
Moderate	37%	19%	19%	7%	7%	10%
Liberal	28%	18%	17%	11%	16%	11%
Religion						
Evangelical Christian	46%	19%	15%	5%	5%	7%
Protestant	41%	24%	17%	6%	5%	7%
Catholic	38%	18%	18%	7%	8%	10%
Other or none	33%	21%	19%	7%	9%	11%
Education Level						
No college degree	37%	22%	17%	5%	7%	12%
Graduated college	39%	18%	18%	9%	8%	8%

	Fewer Than 500,000	750,000	1,000,000	1,500,000	More Than 1,500,000	Not Sure
Income						
Under $100,000	40%	20%	18%	6%	7%	10%
Over $100,000	35%	18%	20%	11%	10%	6%

Rasmussen Reports, 2021. 3,503 likely Hispanic voters. Margin of error, 1.8%.

My favorite question is Poll Question 5: "Recent federal policies have added about one million new permanent immigrants to the United States each year. Which is closest to the number of new immigrants the government should be adding each year" Five numerical answers are presented to the poll taker to choose from, "under 500,000," "750,000," "1 million," "1.5 million," or "over 1.5 million."

I love many things about this question. First, it asks people to choose between real-world scenarios. For 20 years, the Gallup Poll has been asking Americans this pretty vague question: "Are you very satisfied, somewhat satisfied, somewhat dissatisfied or very dissatisfied with the level of immigration into the country today?" If they are dissatisfied, they are asked if they want the level to go up, go down, or stay the same.[173] I've never liked this approach, because most people have no idea how many legal immigrants America already takes each year. Without that numerical context, on what basis will people be able to decide? Also, it's extremely important to use the word "legal" when describing the kind of immigrants we're talking about. If you don't, many people may assume the number includes illegal immigrants. It confuses the issues.

The Rasmussen immigration-level question tells poll takers how many legal immigrants have been arriving each year, and it gives them numerical choices related to options that have been proposed and debated in recent years. When Hispanic likely voters in 2021 learned through the poll question that America already took a million legal immigrants in each year, and they were given several choices of higher and lower levels, plus the option of keeping the same one million a year level, it is instructive that by far the most chosen answer was the *lowest* level of immigration offered.

Thirty-eight percent of all Hispanics want legal immigration set to "under 500,000" a year. That's half the current level! Another 20% want to cut immigration to 750,000 a year, which would be cutting back by a quarter. Together, 58% of Hispanics want to reduce current levels dramatically. Eighteen percent want to keep immigration at a million. Only 15% want immigration levels greater than the current one million a year, currently the position of the Democratic Party. *So, more than three times as many Hispanics want legal immigration to go down as to go up.* Next time you hear a politician pander to a Hispanic audience that while illegal immigration must be eliminated, he/she of course wants to raise the level of *legal* immigration, you can know that politician doesn't actually talk to a broad cross-section of Hispanic voters. Research says Hispanic voters want all kinds of immigration to go down, and for most, go down sharply.

A couple of subgroups had interesting answers. Evangelicals chose the lowest answer, 500,000 a year, by 46%, with 19% choosing 750,000. Those folks want immigration cut dramatically! The same can be said for Hispanics with less than a high school degree. A total of 71% of this category wanted immigration slashed by at least a quarter. Yet is that really a surprise? Aren't the American citizen Hispanics without much education the ones most harmed by large numbers of newly arrived immigrants, all of whom arrive jobless and desperate to work at almost any pay and under almost any conditions?

Poll Question 6: "Do you favor legal immigrants being allowed to bring with them only a spouse and minor children, or do you favor them also eventually bringing in other adult relatives in a process that can include extended family and their spouses' families?"

	Only Spouse and Minor Children	Extended Family	Not Sure
All Hispanics	63%	28%	8%
Gender			
Men	66%	27%	7%
Women	62%	29%	9%

	Only Spouse and Minor Children	Extended Family	Not Sure
Age			
18–39	58%	33%	10%
40–64	**71%**	22%	7%
65+	68%	24%	8%
Party			
Democrat	**59%**	34%	8%
Republican	72%	20%	8%
Independent/Other	63%	27%	10%
Ideology			
Conservative	73%	21%	6%
Moderate	63%	28%	9%
Liberal	53%	38%	8%
Religion			
Evangelical Christian	70%	24%	6%
Protestant	73%	22%	5%
Catholic	61%	29%	10%
Other or none	59%	31%	10%
Education Level			
No college degree	58%	31%	11%
Graduated college	68%	26%	6%
Income			
Under $100,000	62%	29%	9%
Over $100,000	69%	27%	4%

Rasmussen Reports, 2021. 3,503 likely Hispanic voters. Margin of error, 1.8%.

Question number six is about what family members legal immigrants are able to bring with them when the immigrant gets the nod to move to the United States. In 1965, Congress changed the law to give preference to visa applicants with family members already living in the U.S. When people are accepted to come here permanently (green card), they can generally bring in a spouse and minor children as well. So far, no one objects to how this works.

Yet once they have received U.S. citizenship, they are also able to "sponsor" other family members from the home country to come. This includes parents and adult siblings. When those adult siblings come, they can immediately sponsor their own spouses and minor children. When these individuals in turn gain their citizenship, they also can bring in adult siblings. And when the spouses gain citizenship, they can bring in THEIR parents and adult siblings. In this way, admitting one original immigrant can create a "chain" of migration that expands and expands into the indefinite future. In fact, most immigration to the United States is not by people selected for any educational or professional achievement, but because they are simply related to someone already here. Thus, "chain migration" is a frequent target of immigration reformers like me. It epitomizes the mostly random, unplanned approach that drives so many American policies, and especially drives immigration.

Yet every time Congress even talks about cutting back on chain migration, howls of protest go up from those claiming to represent Hispanic interests saying that nothing is more important than prioritizing what they call "family reunification" (chain migration). So, the question is, do Hispanic voters really want this? Do they want people to come to the U.S. based mostly on family connections?

The question is, "Do you favor legal immigrants being allowed to bring with them only a spouse and minor children, or do you favor them also eventually bringing in other adult relatives in a process that can include extended family and their spouses' families?" The answers are "You favor legal immigrants being allowed to bring with them only a spouse and minor children" or "You favor also eventually bringing in other adult relatives that can include extended family and their spouses' families."

The result: 63% of respondents chose to allow legal immigrants to bring in ONLY a spouse and minor children. Just 28% favor allowing them to bring in other adult relatives, what we call the chain migration approach. Even though the Democratic Party advocates increased chain migration entries, Hispanic Democrats and liberals in the poll rejected all chain migration by large numbers. In fact, not a single subgroup of Hispanic voters gave even 40% support to the idea of legal immigrants being able to bring in adult relatives other than their spouse.

Of course, if the current law allows immigrants already here to bring in their adult relatives from outside the country, they will take advantage of this provision, regardless of their opinions about chain migration as a public policy. But try asking one of these individuals if they think the policy of chain migration is good for the United States. I've asked this many times of my immigrant friends, family and neighbors, and almost always, the answer is "No!" When the IRS sent my wife a several hundred dollar "stimulus" check in 2020, she of course cashed it. That did not imply endorsement of stimulus payments as policy.

In the same way, many people assume that anyone whose ancestors benefitted from the U.S. immigration system should not favor it being scaled back. But this idea is built on the logical fallacy that what may have been smart policy in America's past is still good policy today. In the 1950s, lots of people thought it was perfectly ok for their kids to hitchhike. Today, most people would be scared to death if their children did this.

Poll Question 7: "When businesses say they are having trouble finding Americans to take jobs in construction, manufacturing, hospitality and other service work, what is generally best for the country? Is it better for businesses to raise the pay and try harder to recruit non-working Americans even if it causes prices to rise, or is it better for the government to bring in new foreign workers to help keep business costs and prices down?"

	Raise Pay and Hire Unemployed Americans	Import Foreign Workers	Not sure
All Hispanics	64%	22%	14%
Gender			
Men	68%	22%	10%
Women	62%	23%	15%
Age			
18-39	60%	28%	13%
40-64	69%	17%	14%
65+	67%	15%	17%
Party			
Democrat	61%	26%	12%
Republican	70%	17%	13%
Independent/Other	63%	21%	16%

	Raise Pay and Hire Unemployed Americans	Import Foreign Workers	Not sure
Ideology			
Conservative	74%	16%	10%
Moderate	61%	25%	14%
Liberal	59%	26%	15%
Religion			
Evangelical Christian	66%	22%	12%
Protestant	74%	12%	14%
Catholic	61%	26%	13%
Other or none	63%	22%	15%
Education Level			
No college degree	60%	25%	15%
Graduated college	67%	21%	12%
Income			
Under $100,000	63%	23%	13%
Over $100,000	69%	21%	10%

Rasmussen Reports, 2021. 3,503 likely Hispanic voters. Margin of error, 1.8%.

Question 7 asks if worker shortages should be addressed by bringing in more foreign workers to keep costs down, or is it better for "businesses to raise the pay and try harder to recruit non-working Americans even if it causes prices to rise"? When the sample of 3,503 likely Hispanic voters were asked this question across the year 2021, inflation was not yet a big issue. So it's not so surprising that they said that their fellow Americans should be hired even if pay had to rise and prices along with them. The 64% who said businesses should hire Americans and raise their pay to do it got overwhelming support from every subgroup.

The surprise is that polling in July of 2022, when inflation stood at a 40-year high and Americans of all kinds were struggling to pay for gas and food, 60% of Hispanic likely voters were *still* saying that businesses should work harder to recruit non-working Americans *even if* it causes prices to rise! Only 22% wanted to bring in the cheaper foreign workers, even then![174]

Poll Question 8: "Should Congress increase the number of foreign workers taking higher-skill U.S. jobs or does the country already have enough talented people to train and recruit for most of those jobs?"

	U.S. Needs More Foreign Workers	U.S. Has Enough Talent	Not sure
All Hispanics	34%	56%	10%
Gender			
Men	35%	57%	8%
Women	33%	56%	11%
Age			
18–39	47%	43%	10%
40–64	20%	72%	9%
65+	17%	71%	11%
Party			
Democrat	43%	46%	10%
Republican	27%	65%	7%
Independent/Other	24%	65%	11%
Ideology			
Conservative	35%	60%	5%
Moderate	26%	63%	11%
Liberal	39%	48%	12%
Religion			
Evangelical Christian	35%	59%	6%
Protestant	23%	68%	9%
Catholic	37%	52%	11%
Other or none	34%	55%	11%
Education Level			
No college degree	35%	53%	12%
Graduated college	33%	59%	9%
Income			
Under $100,000	34%	56%	10%
Over $100,000	36%	58%	6%

Rasmussen Reports, 2021. 3,503 likely Hispanic voters. Margin of error, 1.8%.

Sometimes even people who favor strict immigration policies say that at least America should at least bring in people with high job skills because they believe we don't have enough skilled people to do those sorts of jobs. How many people believe that? And how many think that the U.S. probably has plenty of people to do most jobs? That is what is asked in poll question 8. Most Hispanic voters reject the idea that we need to bring in highly skilled workers because we do not produce enough. Only 34% say we should bring in more of these workers, as opposed to 56% who say America has plenty of talented people already.

There are a few subgroups that are not so sure, however. Forty-seven percent of voters 18–39 say we need more skilled workers. Curiously, only 20% of those 40–64 said the same thing. Almost half of Democrats also thought America needed imported skilled workers, and so did those without a high school diploma, by 45% to 41%. But strong Hispanic majorities of every religious, educational and income subgroup, along with political independents and Republicans, and voters over the age of 39 agreed that America has plenty of qualified candidates for skilled jobs.

Poll Question 9: "The Census Bureau projects that current immigration policies are responsible for most U.S. population growth and will add 75 million people over the next 40 years. In terms of the effect on the overall quality of life in the United States, do you favor continuing this level of immigration-driven population growth, slowing down immigration-driven population growth or having no immigration-driven population growth at all?"

	Continue Growth	Slow Growth	Have No Growth	Not Sure
All Hispanics	34%	42%	17%	7%
Gender				
Men	33%	42%	19%	5%
Women	34%	42%	15%	8%
Age				
18-39	44%	35%	12%	9%
40-64	21%	51%	23%	4%
65+	24%	49%	20%	7%

	Continue Growth	Slow Growth	Have No Growth	Not Sure
Party				
Democrat	46%	34%	12%	8%
Republican	24%	**50%**	**22%**	5%
Independent/Other	23%	**49%**	**21%**	8%
Ideology				
Conservative	32%	45%	20%	3%
Moderate	28%	48%	16%	8%
Liberal	45%	33%	14%	8%
Religion				
Evangelical Christian	33%	43%	19%	6%
Protestant	29%	45%	22%	4%
Catholic	35%	43%	15%	7%
Other or none	35%	40%	16%	8%
Education Level				
No college degree	34%	40%	15%	10%
Graduated college	33%	44%	18%	5%
Income				
Under $100,000	34%	41%	18%	8%
Over $100,000	38%	45%	15%	3%

Rasmussen Reports, 2021. 3,503 likely Hispanic voters. Margin of error, 1.8%.

The next question asks whether the poll taker is willing to leave immigration levels at their current high level even if it causes the U.S. population to "add 75 million people over the next 40 years." It is a fact that immigration is causing 90 percent of the growth of the population. America had a population of 281,421,906 in the 2000 census. By the 2020 census, just 20 years later, that had grown by 50 million, to 331,449,281. Most of that growth consisted of new immigrants and their offspring. As Pew Research puts it, "Foreign-born Americans and their descendants have been the main driver of U.S. population growth, as well as of national racial and ethnic change, since passage of the 1965 law that rewrote national immigration policy. They also will be the central force in U.S. population growth and change over the next 50 years."[175]

Are Hispanic voters nervous about how this future population growth will affect quality of life? Question 9 shows that this is a consideration for Hispanics, though perhaps not as high as some others.

Forty-two percent said immigration-driven population growth should be slowed to help future quality of life, and another 17% said immigration-driven growth should be stopped altogether. Together, that's 59% wanting to slow or stop population growth even if it means cutting immigration. Only 34% disagreed.

Younger voters, aged 18–39, were not as convinced with just under half (49%) willing to slow immigration-driven population growth for the sake of quality of life, while 44% thought the growth was ok. For middle aged voters, however, aged 40–64, the case seems clearer. Seventy-four percent of them want to slow down or stop immigration-led population growth, with only 21% disagreeing. Democrats were deadlocked on the issue, with 46% wanting to slow down or stop this population growth and 46% wanting it to continue. Republicans and Independent voters were 72% and 70% in favor of slowing or stopping growth, respectively. All religious, educational and income subgroups of Hispanics favored less immigration to slow or stop U.S. population growth.

Poll Question 10: "Should immigration-driven population growth be reduced to limit the expansion of cities into U.S. wildlife habitats and farmland?"

	Yes	No	Not sure
All Hispanics	52%	25%	24%
Gender			
Men	56%	23%	21%
Women	49%	25%	25%
Age			
18-39	57%	25%	18%
40-64	48%	25%	27%
65+	34%	22%	44%
Party			
Democrat	52%	26%	22%
Republican	57%	20%	23%
Independent/Other	48%	26%	27%

	Yes	No	Not sure
Ideology			
Conservative	61%	21%	18%
Moderate	47%	26%	27%
Liberal	45%	31%	24%
Religion			
Evangelical Christian	55%	25%	20%
Protestant	56%	16%	28%
Catholic	51%	27%	22%
Other or none	49%	25%	25%
Education Level			
No college degree	49%	26%	26%
Graduated college	56%	23%	21%
Income			
Under $100,000	52%	25%	23%
Over $100,000	55%	24%	21%

Rasmussen Reports, 2021. 3,503 likely Hispanic voters. Margin of error, 1.8%.

Finally, in question 10, voters were asked whether "immigration-driven population growth" should be cut to keep cities from expanding their footprint into farms and wildlife habitats. All Hispanics said yes by 52% to 25%, with a big 24% unsure. The two subgroups who thought cutting immigration to protect rural lands was most worth it were Conservatives, at 61%, and those who didn't complete high school, who gave a strong 67% backing to this kind of cut.

This environmental-oriented question was the only one of the Rasmussen Index polling that drew a more restrictionist response from younger Hispanic voters (57%) than from the middle-aged (48%) and seniors (34%). Cutting immigration to protect wildlife habitat and farmland was the top choice of every political, ideological, religious, educational, income and age subgroup except Hispanics over the age of 64, whose top choice was "Unsure."

In looking over all 10 questions of this specialized immigration polling, the most striking finding may be how similar Hispanic views are to those of non-Hispanic White voters (whose results are not shown in the tables). Of non-Hispanic White voters, for example, 66% said chain migration should be stopped by admitting only the spouses and minor children of immigrants, as opposed to a bigger group of adult relatives. That's very similar to the 63% of Hispanic voters who felt the same way.

For White voters, 42% wanted legal immigration to be cut by half at least, while 38% of Hispanic voters felt the same way. Only 14% of White voters wanted legal immigration levels to be raised, while just 15% of Hispanic voters thought this. On question after question, the two demographic groups much more agree than disagree. Both groups want more border enforcement, E-Verify, and lower levels of legal immigration. The only real daylight between the two is on the subject of giving amnesty to the broad population of 12 million illegal aliens. Hispanic voters oppose this move very narrowly, with 46% for the amnesty and 49% against. Non-Hispanic White voters are more solidly against this amnesty, with only 37% in favor and 58% opposed.

Democratic Party leaders couldn't be more wrong if they assume that Hispanic voters want the kind of wide-open immigration policies that have characterized Pres. Biden's first two years in office. If anything, the polling data clearly points to Hispanic voter hostility to poorly controlled borders and huge new influxes of foreign workers. Why do Hispanic voters want moderated immigration and strong borders? They want them for the same reasons all other groups of Americans want them.

Hispanic voters are, after all, Americans. Wanting what other Americans want should be expected.

Chapter Ten

The Fiendishly Complex Political Opinions of American Hispanics

Much of today's political writing about Hispanics is wrong or partially wrong simply because the writers don't know enough about Hispanic political opinion.

They try to paint the picture, but without enough in-depth political polling being available, a lot of what political analysts say is of necessity guesswork, the professional equivalent of tea-leaf reading. As I explained in Chapter 9, most political polling of Hispanics is just a crosstab in a wider poll of all Americans. So, in a national poll of 800 or 1,200 or 1,500 Americans, it's rare when much more than a hundred of the persons surveyed are Hispanic. With that small of a sample, no subgroups can be reliably separated.

For this book, we asked Rasmussen Reports to conduct a special poll of only Hispanic likely voters, a big enough poll so that most of the subgroups of Hispanics would be large enough to be scientifically valid with a low margin of error. Although I wanted to ask many political questions, I also wanted enough demographic data about each person polled so that it would suggest the "whys;" that is, not just that someone plans to vote this way or that, but to give enough information about themselves to get at the attitudes behind the political positions.

The poll was conducted in April and early May 2022, and a total of 2,754 were polled. The group polled was balanced by gender, age, region of the country (roughly matching the population of Hispanics in each of the four regions), income level, and political party. The party split was set by the party balance of Hispanics, as revealed by the exit poll of the 2020 presidential election. If it is true that Hispanic party affiliation has shifted in the past two years in favor of the Republican Party, balancing party makeup using the last election, a frequent technique of polling companies, of course will not pick up this shift directly. Indirectly, however, signs of a political migration might be revealed by more Hispanics indicating they plan to vote in the future differently than they did in the immediate past.

Something to keep in mind when comparing answers on the following poll questions is that the two parties are not needing to aim for the same targets. Democrats have traditionally counted on around 70% Hispanic support in order to breathe easy. Polling that breaks close to even tends to predict a likely Democratic disaster. And even a majority of 60% on Democratic issue positions should create uneasiness. Republicans, on the other hand, tend not to need even a majority support from Hispanics. But as shown in the exercise in Chapter 4 about the 2020 Hispanic voting in Georgia, Arizona, Nevada and Pennsylvania, Republicans probably can't feel comfortable until their issues and candidates have the support of around 45% of Hispanics.

Question 1—Biden approval

The first question in the poll is presidential approval: "Do you approve of the job that Pres. Biden is doing?" As for many questions in the poll, possible answers were "strongly approve," "somewhat approve," "somewhat disapprove," and "strongly disapprove."

Overall, 49% either approved or strongly approved. Forty-eight percent either disapproved or strongly disapproved. So, about even. Interestingly, only 21% strongly *approved*, whereas 34% strongly *disapproved*, so the intensity is stronger on the disapproving side. Around the same time this survey was taken, by contrast, another Rasmussen Reports survey found Biden's overall approval with likely voters of every ethnicity to be 42%. Many well-publicized polls published in the summer of 2022 showed Biden's approval numbers falling further still.

As in most of the questions in the poll, there is a significant gender gap. Forty-six percent of Hispanic men approved of Biden's performance, but 52% of women approved. On disapproval, 53% of Hispanic men *disapproved* of Biden's performance in office—only 44%

of women disapproved. And the men's disapproval was stronger, with 41% of men *strongly* disapproving, which is almost as high as the number approving "somewhat" or "strongly" combined. Only 26% of the Hispanic women likely voters "strongly" disapproved.

Poll Question 1: Biden Approval

	Strongly Approve	Somewhat Approve	Somewhat Disapprove	Strongly Disapprove	Not Sure
All Hispanic Likely Voters	21%	28%	14%	34%	2%
Gender					
Men	22%	24%	12%	**41%**	1%
Women	20%	32%	16%	**28%**	3%
Age					
18–29	22%	38%	20%	**18%**	2%
30–39	20%	30%	15%	**31%**	4%
40–64	21%	23%	11%	**44%**	2%
65+	25%	16%	5%	**53%**	1%
Hispanic Identity					
Primary	19%	34%	16%	28%	2%
Secondary	24%	19%	11%	44%	2%
Are you an Immigrant?					
Yes	24%	23%	11%	40%	2%
No	20%	30%	15%	32%	2%
Marital Status					
Married, no children at home	21%	20%	9%	**50%**	1%
Married, w/ children/home	21%	26%	14%	36%	3%
Not married, no children/home	21%	34%	18%	24%	2%
Not married, w/ children/home	20%	35%	15%	28%	2%
Religious Affiliation					
Evangelical	16%	24%	13%	44%	2%
Other Protestant	17%	19%	12%	**52%**	2%
Catholic	22%	28%	15%	32%	2%
Other/None	23%	34%	15%	26%	3%
Religious Attendance					
One or more times per week	24%	21%	7%	**46%**	1%
Couple times a month	22%	26%	14%	37%	1%

	Strongly Approve	Somewhat Approve	Somewhat Disapprove	Strongly Disapprove	Not Sure
Once a month	20%	27%	19%	29%	4%
Several times a year	23%	33%	17%	26%	1%
Rarely or never	17%	34%	17%	29%	3%
Language Spoken at Home					
English	21%	25%	13%	39%	2%
Spanish	27%	31%	13%	27%	2%
Both the same	20%	36%	16%	25%	2%
Political Affiliation					
Republican	14%	11%	12%	62%	1%
Democrat	31%	40%	12%	15%	2%
Other	11%	24%	19%	42%	4%
Political Ideology					
Very conservative	25%	12%	2%	60%	2%
Somewhat conservative	13%	19%	12%	54%	2%
Moderate	18%	31%	19%	31%	2%
Somewhat liberal	23%	43%	17%	14%	2%
Very liberal	40%	37%	12%	10%	1%
Not sure	12%	31%	25%	17%	16%
Education Level					
No college degree	21%	31%	15%	30%	2%
Graduated college	21%	26%	13%	38%	2%
Income					
Under $100,000	20%	31%	15%	33%	2%
Over $100,000	26%	21%	12%	39%	3%

Rasmussen Reports, April 19-May 12, 2022. 2,754 likely Hispanic voters.
Margin of error, 1.8%.

Similarly, there is a clear age gap in the replies on Biden approval, with skepticism increasing at each age level. The starkest differences were in those who "strongly disapprove" of Biden's job performance. Strong disapproval was a very low 18% for Hispanic voters aged 18–29 but rose abruptly to 31% for those in their 30s. Strong disapproval of the job Biden is doing jumped to 37% for Hispanics in their 40s, all the way to 48% for those in their 50s, and finally to 53% for Hispanics who are 60 and older.

There are indications that Hispanic voters who show signs of being more assimilated to U.S. society at large were more likely to disapprove of the President. For example, among Hispanics who say they primarily speak English at home, the majority disapproved (and 37% strongly disapproved) of Biden's job performance, while the majority of voters who primarily speak Spanish at home say they *approved* of Biden.

Another indicator of assimilation is how people answered the survey's questions about ethnic/racial identity. In the polling charts, I show a category labeled "Hispanic Identity" and provide two categories of "Primary" and "Secondary." This is related to questions about identity that are similar to those of the U.S. Census. "Primary" are Hispanics who answered that they are "Hispanic" when asked about their race. "Secondary" are Hispanics who answer the racial question with something else such as "White" or "Black" but, when asked a second question about whether they are of Hispanic ethnicity, they answered in the affirmative. Our survey tables provide a way of determining if there are significant differences between the two groups of Hispanics. Of those whose primary ethnic/racial identity is "Hispanic," just 28% strongly disapproved of Biden's job performance. For those Hispanics who chose White or another race first, strong disapproval was 44%, with 55% disapproving overall.

Interestingly, 40% of Hispanic voters who said they are an immigrant strongly disapproved of Biden's job, while a lower 32% of those who said they are not an immigrant strongly disapproved. This would seem to be an opposite indicator about assimilation. But being an immigrant may not tell us as much as some other indicators about assimilation, since a voter who arrived in the U.S. as an immigrant could have been in the country for five years or five decades. We'll look more at assimilation and political leanings as we go through the poll.

Question 2—Is the government doing enough to stop illegal immigration?

Arguably, the fiscal year 2021 was the worst in U.S. history for illegal border crossings, with 1.6 million illegal border crossers arrested by the Border Patrol as they were entering the U.S. And in the first nine months of fiscal year 2022 (through June 30), arrest levels were up every month over the year previous. Taking just July 1, 2021–June 30, 2022, the Border Patrol nabbed 2.2 million illegal crossers.[176]

Rasmussen asked this question identically in both the 2021 Immigration Index polling and in this special, more political poll of Hispanics. Overall, the answers were similar. In this version, only 15% said the government is doing "too much," while 52% said "too little." Another 25% said the government's efforts to stop illegal immigration is "about right." So, three times as many Hispanic voters think the government is being neglectful as feel it's being overly vigilant.

Poll Question 2: "On the question of illegal immigration, is the government doing too much or too little to reduce illegal border crossings and visitor overstays? Or is the level of action about right?"

	Too Much	Too Little	About Right	Not Sure
All Hispanic Likely Voters	**15%**	**52%**	25%	9%
Gender				
Men	12%	57%	26%	6%
Women	18%	47%	24%	11%
Age				
18-29	26%	37%	29%	9%
30-39	15%	51%	24%	4%
40-64	**7%**	**62%**	23%	7%
65+	12%	61%	16%	11%
Hispanic Identity				
Primary	16%	49%	26%	9%
Secondary	14%	56%	23%	7%
Are You an Immigrant?				
Yes	12%	**60%**	22%	5%
No	16%	**49%**	25%	9%
Marital Status				
Married, no children at home	12%	60%	20%	7%
Married w/ children/home	12%	57%	24%	7%
Unmarried, no children/home	19%	42%	28%	11%
Unmarried w/ children/home	19%	49%	24%	8%

	Too Much	Too Little	About Right	Not Sure
Attendance of Religious Services				
Regularly	14%	58%	23%	5%
Not Regularly	17%	45%	26%	12%
Language Spoken at Home				
English	14%	54%	23%	9%
Spanish	22%	49%	21%	8%
Both	16%	46%	29%	9%
Party				
Democrat	19%	37%	31%	12%
Republican	11%	67%	18%	3%
Independent/Other	12%	**62%**	18%	8%
Ideology				
Conservative	13%	68%	15%	3%
Moderate	11%	**52%**	29%	8%
Liberal	23%	32%	33%	13%
Religion				
Evangelical	13%	62%	19%	6%
Other Protestant	10%	**68%**	18%	4%
Catholic	13%	53%	27%	7%
Other/None	22%	**38%**	26%	13%
Education Level				
No college degree	18%	47%	25%	10%
Graduated college	13%	56%	24%	7%
Income				
Under $100,000	17%	51%	24%	9%
Over $100,000	10%	56%	28%	7%

Rasmussen Reports, April 19-May 12, 2022. 2,754 likely Hispanic voters. Margin of error, 1.8%.

Which Hispanic voters feel this way? As you can see from the table, the choice that the government is doing too little enforcement was the top answer for every subgroup except "liberals" whose top choice was that enforcement was about right (33%), just narrowly higher than "too little" (32%) and quite a bit higher than "too much" (23%). Poll takers who are immigrants themselves were more likely to feel the government was not doing enough (60%). Of American-born Hispanics, a smaller 49% believed the government was not doing enough. Perhaps immigrants who are also citizens and voters are more concerned that others are skipping the line they stood in. A mild surprise is that 37% of Democrats felt the government is doing "too little" to stop illegal immigration. Political independents were very convinced of government neglect, by 63%. This is more evidence that the Biden administration's anemic border controls may be alienating otherwise gettable Hispanic voters.

Completely *un*surprising is how closely this question maps to Biden disapproval. Of poll takers who strongly disapproved of Biden's job performance, 86% also felt that the government is doing "too little" to stop illegal immigration.

Question 3—Is America open and welcoming to Hispanics like you?

Several pollsters of Hispanics have found that this is a very optimistic group of citizens, largely happy with the United States and looking forward with confidence to the future. Our poll found this as well. A strong 43% of Hispanic likely voters felt America is "very open and welcoming" to Hispanics like them. And a further 37% felt it is "somewhat" open and welcoming. Combined, 80% of Hispanics polled felt welcome. Only 14% chose "not very open and welcoming" and a tiny 2% said "not at all open and welcoming."

Poll Question 3: How open and welcoming do you feel the U.S. is to Hispanics like you?

	Very	Somewhat	Not Very	Not at All	Not Sure
All Hispanic Likely Voters	**43%**	**37%**	14%	**2%**	4%
Gender					
Men	47%	35%	10%	2%	5%
Women	39%	38%	18%	2%	4%
Age					
18-29	43%	37%	16%	3%	1%
30-39	42%	37%	15%	1%	4%
40-64	44%	36%	13%	2%	5%
65+	38%	36%	12%	2%	11%

	Very	Somewhat	Not Very	Not at All	Not Sure
Hispanic Identity					
Primary	39%	40%	16%	3%	2%
Secondary	**49%**	**31%**	11%	2%	8%
Are you an Immigrant?					
Yes	56%	33%	9%	1%	1%
No	39%	38%	16%	3%	5%
Marital Status					
Married, no children at home	49%	29%	12%	3%	7%
Married, w/ children/home	44%	39%	13%	1%	4%
Not Married, no children/home	38%	39%	17%	2%	4%
Not married, w/ children/home	41%	39%	16%	3%	2%
Religious Attendance					
Regularly	**50%**	**33%**	11%	2%	5%
Several times a year	42%	39%	16%	2%	3%
Rarely or never	**33%**	**40%**	19%	4%	5%
Religious Affiliation					
Evangelical	49%	32%	13%	2%	4%
Other Protestant	46%	32%	10%	3%	10%
Catholic	44%	38%	12%	2%	4%
Other/None	35%	39%	19%	3%	4%
Language Spoken at Home					
English	43%	36%	14%	2%	6%
Spanish	46%	35%	13%	3%	3%
Both the same	41%	39%	17%	2%	1%
Political Affiliation					
Republican	46%	38%	7%	1%	8%
Democrat	39%	37%	19%	3%	2%
Other	46%	34%	13%	3%	4%
2020 Vote					
Donald Trump	**53%**	31%	6%	1%	8%
Joe Biden	**37%**	39%	20%	3%	2%
Other	34%	43%	14%	7%	2%
Didn't Vote	40%	37%	16%	3%	4%

	Very	Somewhat	Not Very	Not at All	Not Sure
Political Ideology					
Very conservative	61%	24%	6%	1%	8%
Somewhat conservative	48%	35%	9%	1%	6%
Moderate	42%	41%	12%	2%	3%
Somewhat liberal	29%	44%	24%	2%	1%
Very liberal	33%	33%	25%	6%	3%
Education Level					
No college degree	49%	16%	10%	3%	22%
Graduated college	40%	39%	16%	2%	3%
Income					
Less than $100,000	41%	37%	15%	3%	4%
More than $100,000	48%	36%	12%	1%	3%

Rasmussen Reports, April 19-May 12, 2022. 2,754 likely Hispanic voters.
Margin of error, 1.8%.

Does the biggest group of Hispanics, those who felt America is "*very* open and welcoming," differ from the slightly smaller group who thought America is just "somewhat" welcoming? Yes, they were much more likely to say in other parts of the poll that they will vote for Republicans (53%) than Democrats (36%) in the November 2022 general election. And those who said America is only "somewhat" welcoming were much more likely to say they will vote for Democrats (50%) than Republicans (35%). So, if you feel America doesn't like you especially well, you turn to the Democratic Party? This should be studied more. We found that Hispanics who think America is "very" open and welcoming are also most likely planning to vote for Trump over Biden if they both appear on the 2024 ballot, by 51% to 34%, with 9% saying another candidate, the rest unsure. If they felt America is only "somewhat" welcoming, then they plan to back Biden 45%–35%, with 13% wanting somebody else.

A big, big difference of perspective is between immigrants and those born here. Fifty-six percent of Hispanics born in another country chose "very" open and welcoming, but only 39% of those born in the U.S. felt equally welcomed. Perhaps those who have lived in more than one country are better equipped to make this judgment. Combining the answers for "very" and "somewhat" open and welcoming, 89% of immigrants felt a good amount of welcome in America, and a somewhat smaller but still large majority of 77% of American-borns felt welcomed.

Another interesting thing. Fifty-three percent of 2020 Trump voters felt the strongest degree of "very" open and welcoming, but only 37% of Biden voters felt that degree of welcome. Finally, of the poll takers who chose "race relations" as their most important issue, only 21% felt America was very open and welcoming to Hispanics like them—41% said America was "not very open and welcoming."

The overall cheerful view of a welcoming America is further backed up by results of a somewhat similar question asked in June 2022 by Echelon Insights in their poll. When asked whether "America is the greatest country in the world" or whether it was not, 70% of Hispanics said America *was*, in fact, the greatest, against only 23% who said the opposite.[177]

Question 4—Smaller government or larger government?

Every Rasmussen Reports political poll asks takers about their ideology. Are they "very" or "somewhat" conservative, or "moderate," or "very" or "somewhat" liberal? In this poll, 14% said very conservative, 21% said somewhat conservative, 34% said moderate, 16% said somewhat liberal, and another 11% said very liberal.

I got the idea for question four from the Pew Research Center, which asked it in a large 2011 survey of Hispanics residing in the U.S. In the 2011 survey, Pew found that Hispanics wanted bigger government by massive margins, with 75% wanting bigger government and more services against only 19% who chose smaller government with fewer services. However, Pew also checked to see if Hispanics who were second and third generation in this country continued to favor large government. It found that by the third generation, a more modest 58% still favored bigger government.[178]

I wanted to see if we could reproduce the Pew findings. Our methodologies were different in one key respect. Whereas Pew spoke with all Hispanics, citizens and non-citizens, voters and non-voters alike, Rasmussen used their usual technique of polling only regular ("likely") voters, and thus, only citizens. Since this is a book about political shifts, "migrations," I felt only voters really mattered. Also, 11 years had passed since Pew had asked its question, and the U.S. Hispanic population had increased over 20% in that time. Assimilation is further along. Also, 2011 was the age of Obama, and 2022 is the age of Biden, with Trump in between them. The issue needed revisiting.

Poll Question 4: Would you rather have a smaller government providing fewer services or a bigger government providing more services?

	Bigger	Smaller	Not Sure
All Hispanic Likely Voters	**47%**	**41%**	12%
Gender			
Men	**44%**	**47%**	9%
Women	**49%**	**36%**	15%
Age			
18-29	**58%**	**34%**	8%
30-39	47%	36%	17%
40-64	40%	47%	14%
65+	**35%**	**57%**	8%
Hispanic Identity			
Primary	**51%**	**36%**	**14%**
Secondary	**40%**	**51%**	9%
Are you an Immigrant?			
Yes	45%	45%	10%
No	47%	40%	13%
Marital Status			
Married, no children at home	**34%**	**59%**	7%
Married, w/ children/home	47%	42%	12%
Not Married, no children/home	**53%**	**32%**	15%
Not married, w/ children/home	53%	35%	12%
Religious Attendance			
One or more times per week	**41%**	**50%**	9%
Couple times a month	45%	45%	9%
Once a month	50%	41%	9%
Several times a year	**55%**	**32%**	13%
Rarely or never	47%	38%	15%

	Bigger	Smaller	Not Sure
Religious Affiliation			
Evangelical	41%	49%	10%
Other Protestant	40%	54%	6%
Catholic	49%	40%	11%
Other/None	48%	35%	17%
Language Spoken at Home			
English	44%	45%	11%
Spanish	52%	36%	13%
Both the same	52%	35%	13%
Political Affiliation			
Republican	33%	59%	8%
Democrat	61%	26%	13%
Other	35%	52%	14%
Political Ideology			
Conservative	32%	61%	7%
Moderate	48%	38%	14%
Liberal	64%	22%	14%
Education Level			
No college degree	24%	31%	45%
Graduated college	49%	37%	14%
When should abortion be legal?			
Always	64%	24%	12%
Sometimes	39%	51%	10%
Never	29%	62%	9%
Income			
Less than $100,000	47%	40%	13%
More than $100,000	45%	47%	9%

Rasmussen Reports, April 19-May 12, 2022. 2,754 likely Hispanic voters. Margin of error, 1.8%.

In one of the biggest surprises of the survey, only 47% of Hispanic voters wanted bigger government with more services, while 41% preferred smaller government with fewer services, a very narrow split.

That 47-to-41 split in opinions is a remarkable difference from the 75-to-19 split in Pew's 2011 poll. What Rasmussen found on this question was much more in line with the current voting patterns of U.S. Hispanics and may hold important answers to the partisan shifts that have happened thus far. Because the 2011 Pew survey included non-voters and non-citizens, part of the difference in results between 2011 and 2022 can be explained if voting citizens are less likely to look to the government for aid than non-voters and non-citizens. But the almost complete closing of the gap between bigger-government Hispanics and smaller-government Hispanics certainly must suggest a dramatic shift over the last decade on an issue that has clearly divided the two major political parties for most of their history. The 47% of all of today's regularly voting Hispanics who said they prefer a bigger government is even 11 points below what Pew found in 2011 for Hispanics who were at least third-generation Americans!

This Question 4 provides a second measure of political ideology beyond the usual "conservative" and "liberal" labels to help evaluate the other findings from the poll. When Hispanic voters say they are "very conservative," does that always mean they want smaller government? What's the effect of income, education, religion, and geography on the desire for a more activist government? Are those turning to the GOP mostly seeking to change the scope and size of government, or are they equally motivated by other considerations?

Again, there is a non-trivial gender gap. Hispanic male voters, by 47% to 44%, narrowly favored *smaller* government, while female voters supported the concept of bigger government by a 49% to 36% margin. Age is also a big difference. 18–29 year-olds preferred bigger government 58% to 44%. By the time voters hit 65, however, that reverses, with 57% wanting smaller government and only 35% still wanting it to grow.

It's no surprise that 59% of Hispanic Republicans wanted smaller government, as opposed to 33% of them wanting it bigger. Of more significance, I think, is that 52% of those voters not aligned with either party said they want a more modest-sized government with fewer services. Perhaps being an "independent" voter in the Hispanic context may be something like Republican-*leaning.*

For respondents for whom "Hispanic" is their primary ethnic identity, 51% wanted bigger government and only 36% smaller. Whereas for those for whom "Hispanic" is their *secondary* ethnic identity (primary identity is White, Black, or Mixed Race), only 40% wanted bigger government; 51% wanted a smaller one. For those who voted for Trump in 2020, 68% selected smaller government, and only 25%

wanted bigger. For Biden voters, it was nearly the reverse. Sixty-three percent of his voters desired a bigger government with more services, and only 23% wanted a smaller one.

Marriage status also divides neatly on the size of government question. Married people without children at home favored smaller government, 59% to 34%. Married folks with children at home and all categories of unmarried preferred bigger government. One thing that puzzles me were the answers given by people calling themselves "very conservative" and "very liberal." Thirty-one percent of the very conservatives expressed support for "bigger" government and more services, whereas 17% of very liberal people actually said they wanted smaller government. This seems inconsistent to me, and it should be looked into more. Possibly, a significant group of "very" conservative and "very" liberal voters feel social or other issues are more important than the role of government.

Religious affiliation was telling, with Protestants wanting smaller government 51% to 40%, whereas Catholics were very nearly the reverse, desiring a bigger government footprint 49% to 40%. Weekly church attenders favored small government 50% to 41%, whereas those "rarely or never" attending service wanted bigger government 47% to 38% with a large undecided. Social views made a difference. Whereas 64% of those thinking abortion should be "legal under any circumstances" wanted bigger government, those who said it should be "illegal in all circumstances" wanted a smaller government by 62%. Those voters in the middle, who would allow abortion in only some circumstances, also favored smaller government.

Does the language participants speak at home affect what size of government they prefer? Yes. Those speaking mostly English in their homes narrowly favored smaller government, 45% to 44%. If the language at home is Spanish or if they speak English and Spanish about the same at home, they preferred bigger government with more services by 52% to 36% and 52% to 35%, respectively.

Finally, it will be no surprise to anyone that Donald Trump 2020 voters preferred smaller government with fewer services, 68% to 25%, and Joe Biden voters wanted bigger government 63% to 23%. If you strongly approve of Pres. Biden's job performance, you want bigger government, 74% to 16%. But if you strongly *disapprove* of his job in office, then you want smaller government 76% to 17%.

Question 5—Party lean of non-affiliated voters

Though most poll participants were members of a major political party, 771 of them, about a fourth, did not choose either Republican or Democrat. Those individuals were asked, "Do you lean more towards the Republican party or Democrat party?" Thirty-five percent of them said Republican Party, 21% said Democratic Party, and 37% said neither one. This is similar to Independents among non-Hispanic Whites, who have traditionally voted more with the Republican Party. In this poll, Hispanics not aligned with either major party indicated they had voted for Trump over Biden, 43% to 35%, with others going to a third party candidate.

Question 6—Which party are you moving toward?

Poll Question 6: Over the last few years, have you moved closer to the Republican party, the Democrat party, or have you stayed about the same?

	Republican	Democrat	Stayed About the Same	Not Sure
All Hispanic Likely Voters	34%	30%	34%	3%
Gender				
Men	38%	27%	33%	3%
Women	30%	32%	34%	3%
Age				
18-29	26%	37%	34%	3%
30-39	34%	30%	31%	4%
40-64	39%	25%	35%	2%
65+	39%	26%	33%	2%
Hispanic Identity				
Primary	28%	33%	36%	3%
Secondary	**44%**	24%	30%	2%

	Republican	Democrat	Stayed About the Same	Not Sure
Are you an Immigrant?				
Yes	**45%**	26%	27%	3%
No	31%	31%	35%	3%
Marital Status				
Married, no children at home	**48%**	23%	27%	2%
Married, w/ children/home	35%	29%	34%	2%
Not Married, no children/home	25%	32%	39%	4%
Not married, w/ children/home	28%	35%	35%	3%
Religious Attendance				
Regularly	**44%**	16%	33%	7%
Not Regularly	**29%**	24%	41%	5%
Religious Affiliation				
Evangelical	**46%**	24%	27%	3%
Other Protestant	**47%**	21%	32%	0%
Catholic	34%	32%	32%	2%
Other/None	24%	31%	41%	4%
Language Spoken at Home				
English	37%	27%	35%	2%
Spanish	31%	36%	28%	5%
Both the same	27%	36%	34%	3%
Political Affiliation				
Republican	69%	7%	22%	1%
Democrat	14%	53%	33%	1%
Other	36%	12%	45%	7%
2020 Vote				
Donald Trump	71%	5%	22%	2%
Joe Biden	11%	49%	38%	2%
Someone else	23%	18%	53%	6%
Didn't vote	16%	20%	50%	14%
2022 Congressional Voting Intention				
Republican candidate	73%	3%	22%	1%
Democrat candidate	4%	60%	35%	1%
Some other candidate	10%	5%	78%	6%
Not sure	17%	10%	55%	18%

	Republican	Democrat	Stayed About the Same	Not Sure
2024 Presidential Voting Intention				
Joe Biden	5%	56%	36%	2%
Donald Trump	68%	6%	25%	1%
Some other candidate	24%	25%	47%	4%
Won't vote	15%	12%	61%	12%
Not sure	19%	19%	44%	18%
Political Ideology				
Conservative	58%	18%	22%	2%
Moderate	29%	26%	43%	2%
Liberal	11%	50%	36%	2%
Other	12%	20%	42%	25%
Education				
No college degree	10%	18%	18%	54%
Graduated college	28%	31%	37%	4%
When Should Abortion Be Legal?				
Always	19%	42%	37%	2%
Sometimes	42%	24%	32%	2%
Never	50%	16%	31%	3%
Income				
Less than $100,000	32%	30%	35%	3%
More than $100,000	43%	28%	28%	1%

Rasmussen Reports, April 19-May 12, 2022. 2,754 likely Hispanic voters.
Margin of error, 1.8%.

Since this book explores the political journey, the movement, the migration, of Hispanic voters, I thought we should just ask our respondents which party they had been moving toward in the "last few years." Their answers did not clear the matter up much. Thirty-four percent said they had moved toward the Republican Party, 30% said toward the Democrats, and 34% said about the same. So, at least in their overall party identification, there has been no clear movement.

However, men have shifted a bit toward Republicans, with 38% saying they've moved toward the GOP, while only 27% said they've gone more Democratic, with the rest not moving. Women were more static, with 32% saying they've moved more Democratic and 30%

reporting a movement toward the Republican Party. Age groups shed a little more light. Youngest voters, 18–39, have shifted more Democratic, by 34%, while 30% said they've moved more Republican. But 40–64 year-olds showed fairly strong movement toward the Republicans, with 39% moving that way against only 25% going more Democratic. In the oldest group, 65+, it's again 39% moving more GOP, and 26% shifting toward Democrats. Among those Hispanics calling themselves Independents, 36% said they've shifted more Republican, against only 11% saying they are more Democratic.

Marriage is once again a divider on the political question. Both categories of married people have shifted toward the GOP, while both categories of Single have gone the other way.

As in many other questions, religious observance makes a powerful difference in political outlook. Forty-two percent of those who attend religious services of any kind on a regular basis have shifted toward the Republican Party in recent years, while only 28% of them have moved closer to Democrats. For those who don't attend regularly, the case is the opposite, with 53% of them having moved closer to Democrats and only 28% cozying up to the GOP. As the chart indicates, Evangelicals are moving strongly Republican, and Atheists moving dramatically toward the Democratic Party.

Question 7—Who did you vote for in 2020?

The table does the heavy lifting for this question. This poll reports that 37% voted for Trump and 52% for Biden, with six percent saying they voted for another candidate, and 5% did not vote. This is roughly in line with the national exit poll for Hispanic voters, although both numbers may be a bit lower than the actual numbers because 11% of Rasmussen poll participants reported either not voting or voting for a third-party candidate.

Poll Question 7: Who did you vote for in the 2020 U.S. Presidential election? Donald Trump, Joe Biden, someone else, or did you not vote?

	Donald Trump	Joe Biden	Someone Else	Didn't Vote
All Hispanic Likely Voters	37%	52%	6%	5%
Gender				
Men	42%	47%	7%	4%
Women	32%	57%	5%	6%
Age				
18–29	26%	60%	5%	9%
30–39	36%	51%	8%	5%
40–64	42%	49%	6%	3%
65+	54%	42%	3%	1%
Hispanic Identity				
Primary	31%	57%	6%	6%
Secondary	46%	45%	5%	4%
Are you an immigrant?				
Yes	41%	49%	5%	5%
No	36%	53%	6%	5%
Language Spoken at Home				
English	42%	48%	5%	8%
Spanish	38%	49%	4%	9%
Both	33%	51%	6%	11%
Political Affiliation				
Republican	82%	11%	4%	3%
Democrat	9%	86%	3%	3%
Other	43%	33%	13%	11%
Marital Status				
Married, no children at home	49%	43%	5%	3%
Married, w/ children/home	41%	50%	6%	3%
Not Married, no children/home	28%	59%	5%	8%
Not married, w/ children/home	27%	59%	5%	9%
Religious Attendance				
Regularly	44%	46%	6%	4%
Not regularly	29%	58%	6%	7%

	Donald Trump	Joe Biden	Someone Else	Didn't Vote
Religious Affiliation				
Evangelical Christian	53%	36%	6%	5%
Protestant	49%	46%	4%	0%
Catholic	33%	57%	4%	5%
Jewish	49%	51%	0%	0%
Muslim	42%	55%	0%	0%
Atheist	17%	70%	3%	10%
Other/None	33%	55%	8%	7%
Political ideology				
Conservative	67%	25%	4%	3%
Moderate	30%	56%	8%	6%
Liberal	8%	84%	4%	5%
Other	20%	39%	13%	29%
Education				
No college degree	34%	52%	7%	7%
Graduated college	40%	53%	4%	4%
When should abortion be legal?				
Always	19%	71%	6%	4%
Sometimes	46%	44%	6%	5%
Never	58%	32%	6%	5%
Income				
Less than $100,000	35%	53%	6%	6%
More than $100,000	44%	50%	4%	2%

Rasmussen Reports, April 19-May 12, 2022. 2,754 likely Hispanic voters.
Margin of error, 1.8%

Though more Hispanic men voted for Biden than Trump, 47% to 42%, women were more decided Biden voters, supporting him 57% to 32%. Though the youngest voters, 18–29, supported Biden 60% to 26% for Trump, each older age group voted a bit more for Trump until he was the majority in the oldest two groups. Support for Trump grew from 26% among the 18–29 year-olds to 36% for voters in their 30s and 40s, to finally tying with Biden at 46% all for those 50–64, and finally actually winning the 65+ vote by a 54% to 42% margin.

In the Rasmussen poll, the 1,421 college graduates and above participants reported they voted for Biden over Trump by 53% to 40%, with six percent going to another candidate and five percent not voting.

This is significantly *less* Biden support than Pew Research found when they analyzed the 2020 national Hispanic vote; Pew's analysis determined that 69% of college grads supported Biden versus only 30% voting for Trump. On the other hand, our Rasmussen poll shows lower working class support for Trump than did Pew. Rasmussen found that 52% of the Hispanic working class who voted in 2020 supported Biden, and 34% for Trump (the balance supporting a third candidate or not voting). Pew's results were 55%-41% for Biden.

Many times already, this book has referenced Biden winning the Hispanic vote overall, yet some subgroups gave Pres. Trump majority support. If there is a movement among Hispanics toward Republicans, these subgroups are among the vanguard. Who are they? As stated above, older voters chose Trump. So did Hispanic voters who identify primarily as White, Black, or Mixed Race, by 46% to 45%. Those not affiliated with either major party went for Trump 43% to 33%. Evangelical Christians voted for Trump by a decisive 53% to 36%. Other Protestants favored Trump 49% to 46%.

Of special note is the finding that those Hispanic likely voters who think abortion should be "Legal only under certain circumstances" are much more likely to have voted for Trump than average, by 46% Trump to 44% Biden. That is nine points higher than the average Hispanic voter. Of those who believe abortion should *always* be illegal, 58% voted for Trump.

Finally, Hispanics who strongly disapprove of Pres. Biden's performance now also voted against him in 2020—they gave their support to Trump 75% to 16%.

Question 8—The generic Congressional ballot question

One of the standard questions almost every political survey asks is the so-called "generic Congressional ballot" question. It is highly prized by political analysts because it tends to be a fairly accurate measure of which way the partisan winds are blowing in advance of the next Congressional election. Since the question is almost always asked in the same exact way, without using candidate names and instead asking which *political party* voters plan to support during the next Congressional election, it avoids the trap of some poll participants being reluctant to admit they are voting for a candidate they perceive to be unpopular or unacceptable for some other reason.

Poll Question 8: If the elections for Congress were held today, would you vote for the Republican candidate or for the Democratic candidate?

	Republican Candidate	Democratic Candidate	Some Other Candidate	Not Sure
All Hispanic Likely Voters	41%	45%	5%	9%
Gender				
Men	46%	40%	6%	8%
Women	36%	50%	4%	10%
Age				
18–29	32%	53%	6%	9%
30–39	40%	44%	6%	10%
40–64	46%	41%	4%	9%
65+	54%	38%	2%	6%
Hispanic Identity				
Primary	35%	49%	5%	11%
Secondary	51%	39%	4%	6%
Are You an Immigrant?				
Yes	50%	39%	3%	8%
No	39%	47%	5%	9%
Marital Status				
Married, no children at home	57%	34%	3%	6%
Married, w/ children/home	45%	42%	5%	8%
Not Married, no children/home	30%	54%	6%	10%
Not married, w/ children/home	31%	52%	5%	12%
Religious Attendance				
Regularly	51%	38%	4%	7%
Not regularly	31%	53%	6%	11%
Religious Affiliation				
Evangelical Christian	58%	31%	6%	6%
Other Protestant	56%	33%	3%	8%
Catholic	40%	48%	3%	9%
Jewish	39%	50%	11%	0%

	Republican Candidate	Democratic Candidate	Some Other Candidate	Not Sure
Muslim	37%	59%	1%	3%
Atheist	**15%**	**76%**	4%	5%
Other	33%	55%	8%	7%
Language Spoken At Home				
English	45%	43%	5%	8%
Spanish	38%	49%	4%	9%
Both the same	33%	51%	6%	11%
Political Affiliation				
Republican	87%	9%	1%	3%
Democrat	**16%**	78%	1%	6%
Other	**42%**	23%	15%	19%
2020 Vote				
Donald Trump	86%	**7%**	2%	5%
Joe Biden	**12%**	77%	3%	8%
Someone else	31%	22%	32%	15%
Didn't vote	26%	26%	11%	36%
Which Party Do You Trust More on Immigration?				
Republican party	**89%**	**5%**	2%	4%
Democrat party	**4%**	**91%**	2%	3%
Both about the same	25%	34%	20%	21%
Not sure	22%	29%	9%	40%
2024 Voting Intention				
Joe Biden	5%	87%	2%	7%
Donald Trump	85%	7%	3%	5%
Some other candidate	27%	38%	20%	15%
Won't vote	17%	24%	22%	37%
Not sure	21%	27%	13%	40%
Political Ideology				
Conservative	71%	23%	2%	4%
Moderate	35%	45%	7%	13%
Somewhat liberal	16%	73%	4%	7%
Very liberal	9%	83%	4%	4%
Education				
No college degree	37%	47%	6%	11%
Graduated college	45%	44%	4%	7%

	Republican Candidate	Democratic Candidate	Some Other Candidate	Not Sure
When Should Abortion Be Illegal?				
Always	20%	**68%**	4%	7%
Sometimes	**51%**	35%	5%	9%
Never	**67%**	21%	5%	7%
Not sure	26%	42%	7%	26%
Income				
Less than $100,000	39%	46%	5%	9%
More than $100,000	**47%**	42%	3%	8%

Rasmussen Reports, April 19-May 12, 2022. 2,754 likely
Hispanic voters. Margin of error, 1.8%.

Rasmussen found Hispanic likely voters narrowly favoring Democrats for Congress over Republicans by 45% to 41%, with 9% undecided and 5% saying "Some other candidate." Though it's important to point out that there's still LOTS of support for Democrats among Hispanics, constituting a fragile majority, obviously Democrats are losing support with important subgroups and on particular issues.

For several reasons, reaching 41% Hispanic support on the generic ballot is a *great* result for Republicans.

First, actual support for both parties will likely be higher in the actual vote. At this point, the support for both parties together only amounts to 86% of those polled. In the actual election, probably 98% of Hispanic voters will support either the Democratic or Republican candidate(s) for Congress, so support for both parties will probably be higher than the current generic ballot question shows. So, 41% said they had already decided to vote Republican by April-May 2022 when the poll was conducted. The "unsure" group will eventually choose a side to support. If two-thirds of the undecided voters go with the Democrats on election day, and only one-third vote Republican, we could see 53% vote Democratic and 45% vote Republican, with 2% going to minor parties.

Second, this question should cheer Republicans because it represents a *minimum* of four points of extra movement toward the Republican Party since the 2020 election. In Question #7 above, 37% of the

Rasmussen participants said they had voted for Trump two years ago, but 41% said they planned to choose the GOP in the upcoming 2022 election. That is strong forward movement for the GOP, and yet still more movement is likely because of the large group of unsure voters.

Third, this question should cheer the GOP because it contrasts starkly with the Hispanic voting pattern seen in the last non-presidential year Congressional election, held in November 2018. Edison Research conducts the national exit poll for a coalition of media customers. In their exit polling in 2018, they found that 69% of Hispanics voted for Democrats in that election, and only 29% supported Republicans.[179] Republicans did better in the previous two Congressional elections, however. According to Pew Research, Hispanics gave 36% of their votes to the GOP in 2014, and 38% in 2010, both strong Republican years.[180] But neither broke 40%. In fact, Republicans have never received 40% of Hispanic votes in a Congressional midterm election in the 21st century to date, and the Democrats have never gone below 60% support.

If our Rasmussen Reports polling for this book is close to the actual results in the upcoming November 2022 election, with the Democratic share of the Hispanic vote drifting down to the mid-50s, and the GOP winning votes in the low to mid-40s, it will be a tremendous blow to Democratic hopes of containing Republican gains in Congress. Further, it will be a further sign of the Democratic Party being in long-term trouble with the nation's fastest-growing ethnic group.

It's worth noting that of the poll respondents who voted for Joe Biden in 2020, *12% now say they plan to vote for a Republican for Congress* this year, and 8% more are undecided. A smaller 7% of those who voted for Trump now say they will vote for a Democrat for Congress, with 5% undecided. Married people are more inclined to support the GOP in the upcoming 2022 election, with singles sticking with the Democrats. A combined 51% of Protestants voted for Trump in 2020. This year, 57% of them have decided to go with Republican candidates, with 7% undecided and still up for grabs. Only 31% of Protestants so far have decided to vote for a Democrat this fall. It seems almost an understatement to note that if Hispanics become more Protestant as the years pass, Democrats will be hurt by this shift.

For Hispanics who feel that America is "very open and welcoming" to Hispanics like them, 53% have decided to vote Republican this fall, with only 36% decided for Democrats and 7% not sure. For those who say America is "not at all open and welcoming," it is almost the opposite. Only 20% of this alienated population has decided to vote for a Republican, and 58% have resolved to back Democrats, with 14% unsure.

One more note on the generic ballot question. Poll participants who selected the economy as the issue most important to them plan on voting GOP by 57% to 30% this fall, with 9% having not yet decided. If inflation was their number one issue, Republicans would get 54% of those voters. Poll-takers who believe abortion should be legal only under certain circumstances plan to support GOP candidates in 2022 by 51% to 35%. If they think abortion should always be illegal, they favor the GOP this fall, 67% to 21%. On the other hand, if they think abortion should always be *legal*, only one in five (20%) will vote Republican, with 68% planning to choose a Democrat.

Question 9—Which party do you trust on immigration?

Hispanic likely voters were deadlocked on which party they think is better on immigration. Forty percent trust Democrats more, and 39% trust the Republicans. Twelve percent said "both about the same," and 7% felt unsure. So no party has a clear advantage on immigration policy, but there's a lot to learn by studying the subgroups.

Poll Question 9: Which party do you trust more on the issue of immigration, the Republicans or the Democrats?

	Republican Party	Democratic Party	Both the Same	Not Sure
All Hispanic Likely Voters	39%	40%	14%	8%
Gender				
Men	**45%**	**34%**	14%	7%
Women	**33%**	**45%**	14%	8%

	Republican Party	Democratic Party	Both the Same	Not Sure
Age				
18-29	28%	48%	14%	9%
30-39	35%	39%	18%	9%
40-64	46%	35%	12%	6%
65+	52%	33%	9%	5%
Hispanic Identity				
Primary	33%	44%	15%	8%
Secondary	48%	33%	11%	7%
Are You an Immigrant?				
Yes	49%	31%	11%	9%
No	36%	42%	15%	7%
Marital Status				
Married, no children at home	54%	32%	11%	3%
Married, w/ children/home	43%	37%	13%	7%
Not Married, no children/home	26%	48%	16%	11%
Not married, w/ children/home	32%	42%	17%	9%
Religious Attendance				
Regularly	48%	33%	13%	6%
Not regularly	29%	46%	15%	9%
Religious Affiliation				
Evangelical	53%	29%	14%	4%
Other Protestant	55%	29%	11%	5%
Catholic	37%	42%	13%	8%
Other/None	28%	46%	16%	9%
Language Spoken at Home				
English	44%	37%	13%	6%
Spanish	36%	46%	9%	9%
Both the same	28%	45%	18%	9%
Political Affiliation				
Republican	80%	9%	8%	3%
Democrat	14%	70%	11%	5%
Other	42%	17%	24%	16%

	Republican Party	Democratic Party	Both the Same	Not Sure
2020 Vote				
Donald Trump	81%	6%	9%	4%
Joe Biden	11%	69%	13%	7%
Someone else	36%	14%	38%	12%
Didn't vote	20%	21%	29%	31%
2022 Intended Congressional Vote				
Republican candidate	84%	4%	9%	4%
Democrat candidate	4%	80%	10%	5%
Some other candidate	14%	13%	59%	15%
Not sure	19%	15%	32%	34%
2024 Intended Presidential Vote				
Joe Biden	6%	77%	11%	6%
Donald Trump	79%	6%	10%	5%
Some other candidate	25%	31%	32%	12%
Won't vote	18%	28%	30%	24%
Not sure	16%	22%	28%	34%
Political Ideology				
Very conservative	72%	18%	8%	2%
Somewhat conservative	65%	22%	9%	4%
Moderate	33%	37%	21%	10%
Somewhat liberal	15%	66%	13%	6%
Very liberal	9%	76%	8%	7%
Education				
No college degree	33%	41%	16%	10%
Graduated college	44%	38%	12%	5%
Income				
Less than $100,000	37%	40%	15%	8%
More than $100,000	45%	41%	10%	4%

Rasmussen Reports, April 19-May 12, 2022. 2,754 likely
Hispanic voters. Margin of error, 1.8%.

Again, the gender gap is great on this question. Men trust the GOP approach to immigration policy, by 45%-34%. For women, it's the other way around, with them trusting the Democratic Party approach more 45%-33%. Age makes a difference, with younger Hispanics heavily preferring the more permissive immigration policies of Democrats, and older voters preferring the stricter Republicans. Likely voters 18–29 trust Democrats more on immigration, 28%-48%, while voters 50–64 prefer Republicans on this issue 55%-32%.

Those whose primary ethnic identity is Hispanic are tied on the parties at 39% all, while those who identify only secondarily as Hispanics clearly prefer the Republican approach to immigration, 51%-31, as do immigrants, who like the Republicans on immigration 54%-29%. Obviously, Republicans prefer the GOP approach, and Democrats prefer their party. But Independents strongly go with the Republicans on immigration, 52%-14%.

Question 10—Which party do you trust on the economy?

Poll Question 10: Which political party do you trust more on the economy?

	Republican Party	Democratic Party	Both the Same	Not Sure
All Hispanic Likely Voters	45%	36%	12%	7%
Gender				
Men	51%	32%	12%	5%
Women	39%	39%	12%	9%
Age				
18-29	37%	41%	14%	9%
30-39	44%	36%	13%	8%
40-64	50%	33%	12%	5%
65+	54%	31%	11%	4%
Hispanic Identity				
Primary	39%	39%	14%	8%
Secondary	55%	31%	9%	5%
Are You an Immigrant?				
Yes	54%	29%	12%	5%
No	42%	38%	12%	7%

	Republican Party	Democratic Party	Both the Same	Not Sure
Marital Status				
Married, no children at home	60%	29%	8%	3%
Married, w/ children/home	49%	32%	13%	6%
Not Married, no children/home	34%	43%	15%	8%
Not married, w/ children/home	36%	41%	13%	10%
Religious Attendance				
Regularly	54%	31%	10%	5%
Not regularly	36%	41%	15%	9%
Religious Affiliation				
Evangelical	61%	24%	10%	5%
Other Protestant	61%	27%	8%	4%
Catholic	44%	37%	14%	5%
Other/None	33%	43%	13%	11%
Language Spoken in Home				
English	48%	34%	12%	6%
Spanish	40%	43%	10%	8%
Both the same	37%	41%	14%	8%
Political Affiliation				
Republican	85%	9%	5%	2%
Democrat	21%	63%	10%	6%
Other	49%	15%	23%	13%
Political Lean of Indies				
Republican	88%	2%	7%	3%
Democrat	19%	50%	18%	13%
Neither	35%	9%	40%	16%
Not sure	17%	4%	28%	51%
2020 Vote				
Donald Trump	86%	6%	6%	2%
Joe Biden	17%	62%	14%	7%
Someone else	45%	14%	27%	14%
Didn't vote	30%	15%	29%	26%

	Republican Party	Democratic Party	Both the Same	Not Sure
2022 Intended Congressional Vote				
Republican candidate	91%	3%	5%	1%
Democrat candidate	8%	74%	12%	6%
Some other candidate	27%	10%	50%	14%
Not sure	27%	10%	29%	34%
2024 Intended Presidential Vote				
Donald Trump	86%	6%	6%	2%
Joe Biden	9%	72%	13%	6%
Some other candidate	37%	22%	27%	14%
Won't vote	28%	13%	35%	24%
Not sure	30%	13%	23%	34%
Political Ideology				
Conservative	72%	21%	5%	2%
Moderate	**41%**	31%	21%	7%
Liberal	**18%**	64%	10%	8%
Not sure	23%	19%	18%	40%
Education				
No college degree	40%	37%	14%	9%
Graduated college	49%	35%	11%	5%
Income				
Less than $100,000	43%	36%	13%	7%
More than $100,000	51%	38%	8%	3%

Rasmussen Reports, April 19-May 12, 2022. 2,754 likely
Hispanic voters. Margin of error, 1.8%.

The Republican Party has the clear advantage among Hispanic likely voters on the issue of the economy, beating the Democrats 45% to 36%. Many subgroups make the gap even more dramatic. On the economy, men prefer the GOP 51%-32%. Voters who are middle aged and older give majority approval to the GOP, with their support for Democrats on this issue stuck in the 30s. Even 21% of *Democrats* prefer the Republicans to steer the economy. The lack of confidence in the Democrats to handle the nation's economy is appalling among some groups. Only 14% of political independents prefer the Democrats, 29% among married people with no children at home, and 25%

among Protestants. This question is a good indicator of what is behind the opinions of those who strongly disapprove of Biden's job performance; only 3% of them have confidence in Democrats handling the economy. Heck, 18% of political *liberals* prefer the Republican Party's more conservative approach to the economy to that of their own party.

Question 11—Which political issue is the most important to you personally?

Poll Question 11: Which political issue is the most important to you personally?

	All Hispanic Likely Voters	Republicans	Democrats	Other
Economy	36%	47%	31%	35%
Immigration	10%	11%	9%	9%
Healthcare	13%	9%	18%	10%
Education	7%	4%	8%	8%
Inflation	13%	14%	12%	15%
Crime	5%	5%	4%	5%
Race relations	3%	1%	4%	4%
Political unity	2%	2%	2%	2%
Environment/Climate change	7%	3%	9%	8%
Some other issue	3%	3%	3%	4%

Rasmussen Reports, April 19-May 12, 2022. 2,754 likely
Hispanic voters. Margin of error, 1.8%.

Likely voters were given a list of nine issues and a 10th choice of "some other issue" and asked which is the most important to them personally. Fully 36% chose the economy. Nothing else was remotely close. The next two issues in popularity tied at 13% each—inflation and healthcare. There were no real age or gender gaps on the importance of the economy as the number one issue. Strong pluralities of every group agreed that the economy is most important. Among voters who have already decided to vote Republican in the November 2022 Congressional election, 50% say the economy is their most important issue, and an additional 18% said the most important issue was inflation. Together, that means two-thirds of this fall's Hispanic GOP intended voters feel money issues are the most important. In contrast, only 34% of those intending to vote for Democrats chose either one of the two economic issues as most important to them personally.

Question 12—Do you think abortions should be legal under any circumstances, legal only under certain circumstances, or illegal in all circumstances?

The Supreme Court thrust the abortion issue into an even-brighter political spotlight with its decision on June 24, 2022 to overturn the Roe v. Wade decision and give states the authority to set policy. Potentially, Congress could step in and severely restrict or ban abortion nationally. Or, Congress could forbid most or all restrictions to the practice, effectively reestablishing Roe via federal legislation. Since the two major political parties are so diametrically opposite on their abortion views, with the Republican Party wanting to severely restrict the practice and the Democratic Party wanting to make it universally available, the issue has been made, temporarily, at least, more salient than ever for upcoming elections.

The public's views on abortion are so strong that much of American politics has revolved around it for half a century. In fact, a voter's opinion on whether abortion should be legal, and under what circumstances, has become an excellent predictor of which party he or she will belong to and vote for. In varying degrees, it has been a litmus-test issue for both parties, meaning that party loyalty was redefined to include mandatory support for or opposition to abortion.

Poll Question 12: Do you think abortions should be legal under any circumstances, legal only under certain circumstances, or illegal in all circumstances?

	Always Legal	Sometimes Legal	Never Legal	Not Sure
All Hispanic Likely Voters	36%	46%	13%	5%
Gender				
Men	31%	50%	14%	5%
Women	41%	42%	13%	4%
Age				
18–29	46%	40%	10%	4%
30–39	36%	46%	12%	6%
40–64	30%	49%	17%	5%
65+	30%	54%	13%	4%
Hispanic Identification				
Primary	37%	44%	13%	5%
Secondary	34%	48%	14%	4%
Are You an Immigrant?				
Yes	26%	56%	13%	5%
No	39%	43%	13%	5%
Marital Status				
Married, no children at home	31%	50%	15%	3%
Married, w/ children/home	31%	51%	14%	4%
Not Married, no children/home	43%	40%	11%	7%
Not married, w/ children/home	41%	40%	15%	4%
Religious Attendance				
One or more times per week	27%	43%	25%	4%
Couple times a month	28%	51%	18%	4%
Once a month	25%	55%	15%	5%
Several times a year	39%	50%	6%	5%
Rarely or never	48%	41%	5%	6%
Religious Affiliation				
Evangelical Christian	22%	47%	27%	4%
Other Protestant	21%	58%	17%	4%
Catholic	34%	49%	13%	5%
Jewish	36%	56%	7%	1%

	Always Legal	Sometimes Legal	Never Legal	Not Sure
Muslim	50%	32%	15%	3%
Atheist	**73%**	23%	**2%**	2%
Other/None	46%	43%	6%	6%
Language Spoken at Home				
English	37%	47%	12%	4%
Spanish	28%	47%	18%	7%
Both the same	38%	41%	15%	6%
Political Affiliation				
Republican	22%	49%	**25%**	4%
Democrat	49%	**38%**	**9%**	4%
Other	27%	56%	10%	6%
Political Lean of Indies				
Republican	15%	**70%**	13%	2%
Democrat	**50%**	42%	5%	4%
Neither	27%	56%	11%	6%
2020 Vote				
Donald Trump	19%	57%	**21%**	3%
Joe Biden	49%	38%	**8%**	5%
Someone else	35%	45%	14%	6%
Didn't vote	30%	42%	12%	16%
2022 Voting Intention				
Republican candidate	18%	57%	22%	3%
Democrat candidate	54%	35%	6%	4%
Some other candidate	33%	47%	13%	7%
Not sure	29%	47%	10%	14%
Political Ideology				
Very conservative	24%	43%	**29%**	3%
Somewhat conservative	18%	61%	18%	3%
Moderate	34%	49%	**11%**	6%
Somewhat liberal	51%	40%	7%	3%
Very liberal	71%	23%	4%	3%
Not sure	35%	33%	8%	25%
Education				
No college degree	36%	46%	13%	6%
College degree	36%	46%	14%	4%

	Always Legal	Sometimes Legal	Never Legal	Not Sure
Income				
Less than $100,000	37%	44%	14%	5%
More than $100,000	35%	53%	8%	3%

Rasmussen Reports, April 19-May 12, 2022. 2,754 likely Hispanic voters. Margin of error, 1.8%.

Where do Hispanic voters stand? To find out, I requested that Rasmussen ask the question on abortion policy that the Gallup Poll has asked for 50 years. "Do you think abortions should be legal under any circumstances, legal only under certain circumstances, or illegal in all circumstances?" In our poll of 2,754 Hispanics, 36% said it should be legal under any circumstances, while 46% said legal only under certain circumstances, and 13% said illegal under all circumstances.

To compare, Gallup's 2022 polling of registered voters of all ethnicities on the same question, found that 35% answered that abortion should be legal under all circumstances, 50% said only under certain circumstances, and 13% said illegal all the time. As you can see, the answers Rasmussen got from Hispanic likely voters were almost exactly the same as Gallup got from sampling a broad group of registered voters.

Again, as in most other questions, Rasmussen found gender and age gaps. Whereas 46% of 18–29 year-old Hispanics said they want wide-open abortion access, only 28% of 50–64 year-olds wanted it always available. For some of the subgroups, there is a startling difference of opinion on abortion.

Only 25% of Hispanics called themselves Republicans as of the 2020 election, although several recent polls of varying quality show that percentage having ticked up since then. To be cautious, however, our Rasmussen special poll kept the GOP respondents at 25%, with 47% being Democrats. An additional 10% of Hispanic voters are independents but say they lean to the Republican Party. If Republicans are to improve from their one-quarter base, they have to get all of these GOP-leaners, plus they have to pick up true Independents who do not lean to either party. Plus, they have to persuade Democrats who disagree with some of their party's stances to cross party lines on election day.

Religious differences are very telling on abortion policy, with 22% of Hispanic Evangelicals and 23% of Other Protestants saying they support unlimited abortion, as compared to 34% of Catholics and 73% of atheists. On the other end of the spectrum, 27% of Hispanic Evangelicals and 17% of Other Protestants want to ban all abortions, but only 13% of Catholics agree. This finding may shock some readers, since Catholic teaching is so strongly against abortion that obtaining one is considered a mortal sin. For those Hispanic likely voters who attend religious services at least once a week, the percentage who favor making abortion completely illegal nearly doubles to 25%, about the same level of regularly attending Catholics who favor making abortion completely *legal* (27%). For those who rarely or never attend services, only 5% want it banned, with 48% favoring total access.

How will these deep differences affect voting in the upcoming 2022 election? Of those who plan to vote Republican, 18% favor unlimited abortion, and 22% want it totally banned. If voters intend to vote Democratic, by contrast, 54% want total access to abortion, and only 6% want it banned. Our poll was conducted almost two months before the Supreme Court acted to overturn its Roe v. Wade decision. Has the ratcheting up of the stakes on abortion caused those Republicans who want abortion on demand to rethink their party choice? Have those favoring Democrats but who also want abortion heavily regulated or banned now decided that the Democratic Party is not for them? Or maybe no one changes their minds, but one or both parties experience an increase, or perhaps a decrease, in voter interest in actually turning out to vote this fall to express their views on this most contentious of all American political issues.

Question 13—Who will you vote for in 2024 if it's a Biden and Trump rematch?

I love the election rematch question, not because I'm *predicting* these two men will again face each other in the next presidential election, but rather because supposing they will allows voters to express how their views may have changed since the last election. Has there been a shift? If so, in what direction?

Poll Question 13: If the 2024 presidential election was held today, and the main candidates were President Joe Biden and former President Donald Trump, who would you vote for?

	Joe Biden	Donald Trump	Someone Else	Won't Vote	Not Sure
All Hispanic Likely Voters	42%	41%	11%	2%	4%
Gender					
Men	39%	**46%**	11%	1%	4%
Women	**45%**	36%	12%	2%	5%
Age					
18–29	**46%**	**32%**	15%	2%	5%
30–39	44%	38%	11%	2%	6%
40–64	**39%**	**47%**	9%	1%	4%
65+	**38%**	**51%**	9%	0%	2%
Hispanic Identity					
Primary	**46%**	36%	11%	2%	5%
Secondary	36%	**49%**	11%	1%	3%
Are You an Immigrant?					
Yes	38%	49%	8%	1%	4%
No	43%	39%	12%	2%	4%
Marital Status					
Married, no children at home	**35%**	**52%**	10%	0%	3%
Married, w/ children/home	39%	45%	11%	2%	4%
Not Married, no children/home	49%	31%	13%	2%	5%
Not married, w/ children/home	**47%**	**33%**	12%	2%	6%
Religious Attendance					
One or more times per week	36%	**50%**	10%	1%	4%
Couple times a month	36%	**52%**	8%	1%	3%
Once a month	38%	44%	9%	1%	8%
Several times a year	**46%**	32%	15%	2%	5%
Rarely or never	**49%**	32%	12%	2%	5%

	Joe Biden	Donald Trump	Someone Else	Won't Vote	Not Sure
Religious Affiliation					
Evangelical	28%	57%	10%	1%	3%
Other Protestant	33%	51%	11%	1%	4%
Catholic	44%	41%	9%	2%	5%
Other/None	50%	29%	14%	2%	5%
Language Spoken at Home					
English	40%	44%	11%	1%	4%
Spanish	46%	41%	7%	2%	4%
Both the same	45%	34%	13%	2%	6%
Political Affiliation					
Republican	12%	77%	7%	0%	3%
Democrat	69%	18%	10%	1%	3%
Other	24%	47%	18%	3%	8%
Political Leaning of Indies					
Republican	3%	82%	10%	1%	3%
Democrat	58%	14%	18%	3%	7%
Neither	24%	37%	25%	6%	8%
Not sure	23%	22%	16%	4%	35%
2020 Vote					
Donald Trump	4%	88%	5%	0%	3%
Joe Biden	74%	11%	11%	1%	3%
Someone else	14%	20%	49%	2%	14%
Didn't vote	19%	30%	20%	11%	20%
2022 Intended Congressional Vote					
Republican candidate	5%	85%	7%	1%	2%
Democrat candidate	81%	6%	9%	1%	3%
Some other candidate	13%	23%	45%	7%	12%
Not sure	31%	24%	19%	6%	19%
Which party do you trust more on immigration?					
Republican party	6%	84%	7%	1%	2%
Democrat party	81%	6%	9%	1%	2%
Both about the same	34%	29%	25%	3%	9%
Political Ideology					
Conservative	23%	67%	7%	1%	2%
Moderate	41%	36%	15%	2%	6%
Liberal	70%	15%	12%	1%	2%

	Joe Biden	Donald Trump	Someone Else	Won't Vote	Not Sure
Education					
No college degree	43%	38%	11%	2%	5%
Graduated college	41%	43%	11%	1%	4%
When Should Abortion Be Legal?					
Always	62%	19%	14%	1%	3%
Sometimes	33%	52%	10%	2%	4%
Never	19%	66%	9%	2%	5%
Income					
Less than $100,000	42%	41%	11%	2%	5%
More than $100,000	43%	42%	11%	1%	3%

Rasmussen Reports, April 19-May 12, 2022. 2,754 likely Hispanic voters. Margin of error, 1.8%.

From the other questions in this poll, probably no one will be surprised that Donald Trump would receive somewhat more support for president in the hypothetical rematch, and Joe Biden would get sharply fewer votes. Among Hispanic likely voters, only 42% now say they would vote for Biden next time, while 41% say they would vote for Trump. Eleven percent wish they could choose someone else, and 4% say they are unsure. Only 2% already assert that they would not vote if those candidates are their choice.

The movement toward Trump is four points, from 37% of those who said they voted for him in 2024 to 41% who say they will do so if there's a rematch. Yet since 11% answered they'd vote for "some other candidate," it is possible that a different Republican candidate might receive more votes from Hispanics than the portion who now say they'll vote for Trump. So, the news for Republicans is good. If Trump or another Republican received 41% or more Hispanic support, that would be the highest level in this century, and perhaps ever. Possibly, it would be enough to deny the Democrats the White House if a battleground state like Nevada or Arizona, with many Hispanics and where Biden barely won in 2020, were to tip to the GOP because of more Hispanic support for the Republican candidate.

The news for Biden and the Democrats is not at all good. In our poll, 52% said they had voted for Biden in 2020, but only 42% said they would do so if there were a rematch. That's a loss of 10 points—about 20% of his former support. If that were actually to happen, together with a four-point or greater pickup of support for Trump in this theoretical rematch, Joe Biden would almost certainly lose.

Once again, there are strong gender and age gaps. Women prefer Biden, and men prefer Trump in this hypothetical scenario, but neither yet enjoys the majority support of either group. Though 46% of 18–29 year-olds say they'd vote for Biden, that shrinks to 36% for the 50–64 year-olds. In the same age groups, Trump gets only 32% of the young voters but a big 52% of the older group say they would go for Trump the next time.

Twelve percent of Republicans say they'd break ranks and vote for Biden, yet 18% of Democrats state they would vote for Trump. Those voters not identifying with either major party lean strongly to Trump, saying they'll support him by 47%, against only 25% having decided for Biden. A big group, 18%, wants other candidates.

The worst news for Democrats, perhaps in the whole poll, is that 11% of those who voted for Joe Biden in 2020 now say they'll vote for Trump, as against only 4% of Trump voters who say they'll vote for Biden next time.

Eighty-eight percent of Trump voters say they'll stick with their man, but only 74% of former Biden voters say the same. For those married people with no children in the home, 52% say they will vote for Trump and only 35% declare for Biden. By contrast, those who are unmarried but have children at home say they'll vote for Biden in 2024 47% to 33%. Evangelicals plan to vote for Trump if he's on the ballot, 57%—28%. Catholics narrowly favor Biden if there's a next time, 44%—41%.

Other subgroups come out as expected, as the chart shows, but there is one curious surprise in the Rasmussen data. A few other studies of Hispanics, but notably Pew Research's analysis of 2020 voting, found that Hispanic working class voters, those without a four-year college degree or more, were much more supportive of Trump than were college grads. Our poll found something like the opposite. In the earlier question asking which candidate did they vote for in 2020, only 34% of the working class said they had voted for Trump, whereas 40% of those with a college degree and above said they voted for him.

Similarly, working class voters said that if their choice for president in 2024 is again Biden versus Trump, they'll support Biden 43%—38%. Forty-one percent of college grads said they'll vote for Biden, but 43% said Trump will get their vote. Donald Trump will pick up support with both groups if he runs again, according to our Rasmussen results, and perhaps that should be the bottom line. We don't know whether different candidates for the two parties in 2024 would change this picture. But at least for now, the clear shift is in the GOP direction.

Chapter Eleven

Where the Political Migrants Are Heading: Poll-Driven Advice & Predictions for Both Parties

T his book is about the political migration of Hispanic voters from being a group newly arrived in America, not very assimilated, fairly reliable Democratic Party voters, to the country's largest ethnic minority, mostly born here, growing in confidence, and up for grabs politically.

After reviewing all the polling and other data available and living with this question during the lengthy process of researching and writing this volume, I have some advice for leaders of both of the major political parties. In this last chapter, I'll share what I think the data suggests about how they can secure the most possible loyalty and votes from Hispanic voters now and on into the future.

Advice for the Republican Party

Whether by lucky trial and error or by really understanding how to win the affection of Hispanic voters, Republicans have all the momentum right now. Here are my thoughts on how to keep it going.

Play up the border

Especially as long as Democrats control the White House, Republicans should talk about the chaos at the U.S. Mexico border nonstop. Never forget that *all* Hispanic voters are United States citizens, most born in this country. They know whose side they are on. Border control is not

Americans against immigrants. All Americans, including Hispanics, and yes, immigrants, are against chaos, crime, drugs, and those who would endanger our children. Hispanic Americans are more likely than any other group to live in communities across America most afflicted by those results of a poorly enforced border. Drugs coming in from Mexico are a huge turnoff to all voters. Emphasize that the only way to keep our vulnerable youth safe from gangs is to control the border.

There are so many angles here that work. Emphasize that border lawlessness puts Border Patrol agents in danger every day. Show lots of photos in ads of smiling Hispanic Border Patrol agents. In political rallies held at border states, make it a habit to have Hispanic sheriff's deputies, police officers, and Border Patrol agents on the platform to remind everyone that Hispanic Americans serve on the front line protecting this country. Remember that a solid majority of Hispanic likely voters believe that the Biden administration has bungled its handling of the border and has done far too little to get it under control. Don't demonize the illegal border crossers, and especially take care to avoid the harsh rhetoric that Pres. Trump sometimes used about those from Mexico; keep the criticism on those who are making and carrying out the bad policies.

Talk up E-Verify. Remind people that there is a way without pain to reserve U.S. jobs for those in the country legally. Emphasize that greedy employers want to undercut American workers of every ethnicity by hiring cheap illegal workers who just arrived across the border. Our poll and every poll demonstrate that E-Verify is a winner with every type of voter. Standing up to the cheap labor advocates on this issue is an excellent opportunity to break the stereotype of Republicans turning their backs on regular working people to do the bidding of business lobbies. And E-Verify is a way to fight illegal immigration without having to rely on a heavy deportation program which is not particularly popular with Hispanics.

Above all things, Republicans should resist the urge to pander to Hispanic audiences about immigration. Although Hispanics are proud of their heritage and glad for their families and countrymen who came to the U.S., that doesn't mean they think *high rates* of immigration continue to help this country. The 2013 Republican "autopsy" report advising mass amnesties and increases in immigration as the way to reach Hispanics has been soundly discredited. Fifty-eight percent of Hispanic likely voters think annual immigration numbers should be *cut,* and only 15% believe America should *increase* the numbers. Republicans will hit the mark with Hispanic audiences if they say America should bring in new immigrants when it helps this country but that our first duty is to ensure opportunity and security for Americans of all ethnicities already here.

Be bullish about America

One clear finding of our special Rasmussen poll, and of polls conducted by others, is that most Hispanics are upbeat about their experience in America and optimistic about their future here. Hispanics believe in America. They heavily serve in our armed forces, with 21% of active duty servicewomen being Hispanic and 18% of active duty servicemen. I think one appeal Donald Trump has for Hispanics who back him is his bullishness on America. Republicans should continue to emphasize the good America does, both here and around the world. Admit that America has problems while showing eagerness to face and overcome them.

Recall that 80% of Hispanic voters feel that America is open and welcoming to "Hispanics like me." But also recall that this doesn't necessarily mean that they feel welcoming toward *illegal* immigrants. Personally, they may know and accept individuals within their orbit who are illegally present, but they know that illegal immigration is a bad thing for America.

Remember that the core of your Hispanic audience is religious

Only a portion of American voters are strongly religious, but those who are do lean very decidedly toward the Republican Party. There are many reasons why this is, and the list of issues is only growing as time goes by. Gallup's latest study of church membership among Americans shows that 65% of Republicans belong to a church body, whereas only 46% of Democrats do.[181]

Our Rasmussen Reports survey for this book found that 58% of Hispanic Evangelicals and 56% of Other Protestants plan to vote for Republicans in the November 2022 Congressional elections, while 40% of Catholics said they would support the GOP. Refining this to regular attendees of any kind of religious service, 54% said they plan to support Republicans, as opposed to only 31% indicating they had decided to back Democrats. Republicans tend to already have built-in appeals to religious people through an openness to talk about religious principles.

Middle aged voters are your natural allies

Our polling shows support for Republicans and conservative issues strongest among voters 40 and older. Although Hispanic likely voters aged 18–39 are basically unsure about which party they trust more on economic matters, voters 40–64 choose the Republican Party on matters of the economy by 50%–33%. Voters 65 and older feel even stronger about it. Although overall Hispanic voters plan to vote Democratic this fall by a fairly narrow margin of 45%–41%, with many undecided, voters 40–64 see it very differently, planning to vote GOP by 46%–41%. Those 65+ plan to vote Republican by 54%–38%!

Don't forget that a third of the youngest voters are for you

It's very true that young Hispanics, like young people of every ethnicity in America, are much more Democratic in orientation. In general, they take progressive stands on social issues like gender and abortion. They are much more willing to back amnesties.

Yet, as I discovered when researching voter attitudes on immigration, at least a third of young people lean conservative. This group may well be more religious than the average of their age group—I'm not certain. However, this group of what I call "natural conservatives" does favor sharply curtailed legal immigration (26% of 18–29-year-olds want to slash it by half), trusts the GOP more on the economy (37% feel this way), desire *smaller* government (36% want this!), and a quarter of them say they are moving closer to the Republican Party.

This translates nicely to their voting intentions. Although only 26% of this youngest group in our poll voted for Trump in 2020, 32% say they will vote for GOP candidates this fall. That's a *six-point pickup*, or about a 20% improvement from the previous election.

How can Republicans best appeal to young voters? Forty-three percent of those 18–29 feel that America is "very open and welcoming" to Hispanics like them, with another 37% believing it is "somewhat" open and welcoming. Together, that means that 80% of young Hispanic likely voters have a positive image of America's acceptance of them. Young people are optimistic and future-oriented. So Republicans need to talk about how great America is in being able to bring people together from around the world and make of them one people.

Everything we know about Hispanic people in America reinforces that they are all about hard work. They want to work, and they are not afraid of working very hard. Don't treat them as victims; their history doesn't support that. Emphasize that America is the land where work is plentiful and where work is rewarded! Talk about how America makes self-improvement easy.

Win over the women

Republicans are much weaker with Hispanic women than with men. According to our poll, 42% of Hispanic men voted for Donald Trump's reelection in 2020, but only 32% of women did so. But the news gets better from that point. Catalist, the Democratic Party-aligned data research organization, in its research into the 2020 election, said that the biggest group of Hispanic voters to move to the GOP from the Democratic Party was actually women. According to *Politico*'s writeup of the Catalist research, the "likeliest Latino voters to swing away from Democrats from 2016 to 2020 were younger, female and those without a college degree—subsets that usually trend bluer. The research also showed that the greatest deterioration came among Latinas [women]: From 2016 to 2020, support for Democrats among Latinas dropped by 11 points compared to Latino men, whose support for Democrats declined by 6 points."[182]

As our Rasmussen Research poll of Hispanic likely voters found, there is a significant gender gap between men and women on most questions asked, with Hispanic women being more likely to support Democratic positions. Yet that gap is narrowing. To overcome a similar gender gap with non-Hispanic White women that had opened a few decades ago, Republicans began to run many more female candidates for Congress and state races. This has proven successful, and now Hispanic women are running for Congress in higher numbers.

One example of this is in the Rio Grande Valley of South Texas, where three GOP women are running for House seats that are all now controlled by Democrats. In my spring 2022 sojourn to the southern border, I met with two of the women. One, Monica De La Cruz, is a polished, highly energetic businesswoman running for an open seat in the Texas 15th Congressional District, which begins at the Rio Grande River and runs up in a narrow stack of counties to the San Antonio suburbs. We met Monica in McAllen, Texas, at the "Hispanic Community Center," one of several such facilities the Republican National Committee has opened around the country in advance of the 2022 election. Monica strikes the visitor as extremely energetic and organized, a seasoned political hand.

In 2020, De La Cruz came within 7,000 votes of knocking off Democratic incumbent Vicente Gonzalez. After his narrow escape and a post-Census redistricting, the Democrat decided to run in a neighboring district this fall. The Texas legislature redrew the Texas 15th for this election to be two points more Republican this year, which is now evenly divided between Republican and Democratic voters.[183] Monica should be a strong favorite in the fall, since this is shaping up to be a very Republican year, *and* she is not running against an incumbent this time, *plus* her name is now well known in the district.

What issues is she running on? A Youtube video placed prominently on her campaign's website's homepage makes that clear. "Almost two-thirds of our border is unsecure. You have to see it to believe it," she tells the camera before entering a helicopter to tour the border. "Socialists are ruining our border security, our values, and our economy," she says while the copter passes over sections of the border wall. I expect her to win handily.

The case of Mayra Flores

Next door, in Texas 34, my group met candidate (and now U.S. Representative) Mayra Flores. Mayra's photos show a very sweet-looking youngish woman. She asked that we meet her at a coffee shop called "He Brews Life," run out of the New Life Family Church, an evangelical non-denominational body in McAllen. New Life holds all its services in English, which shows how far assimilation has reached in this 87% Hispanic town. In person, Mayra seemed even younger and more humble than in her photos. But her campaigning style is very tough and right-leaning, with plenty of quips and barbed sound-bites about Democrats.

When we met with her in the first week of April, Mayra had just learned that the sitting Democratic Congressman in the 34th District, Rep. Filemon Vela, had resigned to take a Washington lobbying job. (Almost immediately, Mayra announced that she would run in the special election to fill the remaining few months of his term. In June, she won that race and is now preparing to defend her seat in a redrawn district, now more Democratic and probably harder to win.)

While sipping my coffee, I asked Mayra if she attended the church. She told me it was *one* of the churches she attended. In fact, she is an evangelical with very deep roots in the Evangelical community of the Rio Grande Valley and was heavily backed by them. The daughter of migrant farm workers, Mayra was born in Mexico but moved to Texas as a child. She picked cotton as a teenager with her parents, becoming a U.S. citizen along the way. She is married to a Border Patrol agent and started off as a Democrat. However, the progressive views of the Democratic Party, especially on abortion, turned her off, and she became a Republican voter, then activist and leader. Her campaign slogan was "God, family, country," and she says this represents the traditional views of her constituents.

When she took her seat in June, she became the first Mexico-born woman ever to serve in Congress. Her pastor came to Washington to attend her swearing-in. As if to confirm how different she is from the usual newly elected member of Congress, Mayra tweeted out in early July, "I am an Ambassador of Christ and becoming a Congresswoman doesn't change that. Our Country belongs to God not a political party. I am here to win souls for God. Hallelujah".[184] On July 6, *The New York Times* ran a profile of the three Hispanic women running for Congress in the Rio Grande Valley titled, "The Rise of the Far Right Latina."[185]

As far as I can see now, Republicans are generally on the right course to extend their reach with America's Hispanic voters. Candidates like Mayra Florez may seem exotic to readers of New York newspapers, but there's a big audience for her brand of politics in Hispanic South Texas. As I have emphasized in earlier chapters, all Hispanic communities are not alike. But the Hispanic women running for office in the Rio Grande Valley offer a template to consider for Republicans trying to at least reach that next goal of 45% Hispanic voters: Emphasize Border security and moderate immigration policies, be tough on crime, be optimistic and patriotic about America, talk about faith, concentrate on your core of middle-aged supporters while cultivating the more conservative young voters, and finally, put women out front as often as possible. America's Hispanics will come to you.

Advice for the Democratic Party

For a couple of decades, political analysts have talked about similarities between Hispanic immigrants of this era and Italian immigrants of a century ago. They have speculated about whether and how fast Hispanics might resemble Italian immigrants and their descendants in their many-decades-long transition from Democratic stalwarts into reliable Republican voters by mid-20th century. By 2016, it was difficult to imagine that Italian Americans had once been such a rock solid immigrant cornerstone of the Democratic voting bloc. That year, for example, a poll run by BuzzFeed News found that Americans who identified most strongly with their Italian or their German heritage were the strongest supporters of candidate Donald Trump![186]

And 2016 was also the year when election results showed the first hint that Hispanics might be getting started on the Italian political-journey storyline. Then, the 2020 exit polls turned that hint into boldfaced headlines, as I discussed in earlier chapters.

Since then, one Democratic strategist or commentator after another has been issuing urgent warnings to party leaders to not lose another immigrant group, one that has long offered Democrats a voter majority the party cannot afford to lose. You have read their recommendations throughout the book. You have also read about a plethora of polling that tends to back up their recommendations.

Those recommendations look pretty convincing to me. It is not inevitable that the Democratic Party will lose its majority appeal among Hispanic voters. Here is some advice to Democrats on how to keep that majority.

Mute all talk of socialism

One of the things that is hurting Democrats with Hispanic voters the most is the perception that the party may be moving closer to socialism. According to EquisResearch's postmortem on the 2020 election, Republican attacks on Democrats being socialists really broke through. The socialism charge got through to "Latino voters who most believe in social mobility through hard work—consistent with the idea that, in the right-wing narrative, the true opposite of socialism is the American Dream," says the report. "While the socialism attack rings various bells, the through-line among those concerned is a worry over people becoming 'lazy & dependent on government', by those who highly value 'hard work.'"[187]

Hispanic voters' responses to Question 4 in the survey for this book ring a warning bell that a tipping point might be approaching on a key ideological issue. The question was: "Would you rather have a smaller government providing fewer services or a bigger government providing more services?"

Ever since the small Hispanic population of the 1960s has exploded through the renewal of mass immigration, it has always been assumed that Hispanics' answer to that question is overwhelmingly "BIGGER." Research has suggested that every immigrant group from nearly every country to nearly any other country tends to be more in favor of bigger governments than the native-born citizens of the receiving country. Thus, immigrant groups usually favor the political party in a country that is more in favor of bigger government services. There has been little reason to think that the United States' booming immigrant population from Latin America would be an exception.

The Pew Research Center survey of 2011 indeed found Hispanics favoring a bigger over a smaller government by 75% to 19%. Three-quarters of all Hispanic respondents in 2011 said they preferred a bigger government providing more services.

But as I noted in Chapter 10, the 75-to-19 margin of 2011 had shrunk to a 45-to-41 margin in the 2022 Rasmussen Reports poll that used the exact Pew wording in its question! With that speed of change, are we nearing the tipping point where the majority of Hispanic voters actually favor a smaller-government ideology?

This change already may be a major factor in the willingness of significant additional numbers of Hispanics to take a look at a Republican Party which has never been part of their tradition. For decades, observers have questioned why an Hispanic population that tends to be more culturally conservative would continue to vote overwhelmingly for a Democratic Party whose national platform has been moving more culturally progressive. A common explanation is that His-panics' strong preference for a bigger government is more important to them than their conservative cultural views and is the ideological fence that keeps Hispanics in the Democratic fold. But as the Hispanic preference for bigger government weakens, and perhaps moves into a minority position, will that "fence" collapse?

The Democratic Party certainly isn't going to become the party that is the biggest champion of smaller government and services. But to hold on to enough of the Hispanic Democrats who are moving in that direction, you need to be clearer that your leaders who describe them-selves as socialists or who advocate what they identify as socialist policies are only a wing of the party and not a major influence. Maybe you aren't willing to do that; you may feel that the main energy and the proper direction for the country is for the Democratic Party to become more leftist. But if holding on to your Hispanic majority is a major party priority, muting the socialist and socialist-type rhetoric appears to be an important, probably essential, tactic.

EquisLabs asked 2020 Hispanic voters which of the following they were more concerned about: "Democrats embracing socialism/leftist policies," or "Republicans embracing fascist/anti-democratic policies."

A truly solid Democratic base would have mostly feared the Repub-licans. But Hispanic voters were almost equally divided: 42% were more worried about Democrats embracing socialism, while 38% were more worried about Republicans and fascism.

Toying with socialism may energize a portion of the left-leaning Democratic base, but it is a terrible turnoff to mainstream Hispanics, who prize hard work above all else and who hate the socialism that many of them have observed directly or indirectly in Cuba, Venezuela, and other places.

Treat Hispanics first as Americans

To keep the majority of Hispanic voters in the Democratic fold, you need to stop treating them primarily as an immigrant population and shift to a native-born citizen approach. Don't treat them as outsiders or victims or newcomers but as fully participating and contributing Americans.

Even though Hispanic immigration to the United States continues at a blurring pace, most Hispanics today are citizens. And most Hispanic voters were born in this country. Assimilation is moving along pretty smartly. The English language takes over in time, as has been the case for previous waves of immigration. Hispanics resent chaos at the U.S. Mexico border, just like most Americans. They are affected by labor market trends, just like all Americans. They love this country and are happy to be here. They are family oriented and like traditional values. To me, Hispanic Americans of today are reminiscent of Italian Americans of the mid-20th century, and look where *they* ended up voting by the 1980s.

The crosstabs on the 2020 bigger-vs.-smaller government question provide insight into the direction that assimilation appears to be taking Hispanic Americans. Those who primarily speak Spanish at home preferred a *bigger* government by a 52–36 margin. But those who primarily speak English at home were evenly divided (preferring *smaller* government and services by 45–44). The latter group will only continue to become a larger percentage of Hispanic voters.

The way that Hispanics see their identity makes an even greater difference. Those who said "Hispanic" was their *secondary* identity (and not their racial identity) preferred *smaller* government by a 51–40 margin. In general, older Hispanics have lived in the United States longer than young adults; their answers may also suggest a trend. Middle-aged Hispanic voters (age 40–64) preferred smaller government by 47–40, while Hispanic seniors preferred smaller government by 57–35.

Those trends won't necessarily continue, but they look robust. As noted in the previous section, without a strong preference for the Democratic Party's ideology of bigger government and services, Hispanics' social positions may become more influential in how they vote. To the extent that those social positions are different from the dominant Democratic stance, you need to consider making a bigger tent. That doesn't necessarily mean you have to change the party stance on an issue, but you need to at least leave room for Democratic voters and elected officials to take differing positions at times. A sign of respect for social, religious, and cultural differences could be very helpful in holding your Hispanic majority.

The foundation of the Democratic Party's voter appeal is that it seeks to make life more fair for Americans. Your party has always been the primary champion of social welfare for new immigrant populations. This has been a part of why your party has always seemed the natural home of Hispanics. But with most Hispanic voters moving generations away from their immigrant roots, their concerns are more and more typical working class concerns of fairness for those who do the work, take care of their families, and pursue their individual ideas of freedom. You'll likely have little trouble continuing to do well with newcomers, but the majority native-born Hispanics need a modified approach.

Sound as happy to be an American as most Hispanics are

This is a great, great country—that's why millions of immigrants from Hispanic homelands left everything behind to get to America, and why they continue coming in enormous numbers. America is the land of dreams, the place where when you call the police, they come! When you lose your job, you collect relief benefits! When you are desperately ill, you go to the hospital and they treat you no matter what's in your bank account! If you want to start a church, you start one! If you are poor but work hard and get good grades, scholarships are usually available to attend a college.

Fall in love with this country again. Praise it in every one of your speeches. Don't sound world-weary. Don't be so negative! Don't dwell on America's past mistakes. Rather, emphasize our brilliant future! Hispanics in America respond to hope and smiles and uplift!

Remember that 80% of Hispanic voters feel that America is open and welcoming to "Hispanics like me." Do Democrats want their brand to be dominated by Hispanic leaders like Rep. Alexandria Ocasio-Cortez, who said about the Bronx in New York City, "I was born in a place where your ZIP code determines your destiny"?[188] If so, only the 16% of Hispanic likely voters who feel America is *not* open and welcoming to Hispanics like them may be listening.

Move to an American worker-oriented immigration policy

Yes, most Hispanics come from families that moved to America just one or two generations ago. That means they are still insecure here. One way things can go sour for people trying to establish themselves is by tons more immigrants moving in and taking jobs at lower wages. Nobody wants this to happen. As our polling shows, Hispanics want to take many steps to discourage illegal immigration and to keep legal immigration at moderately low levels. This is not about ethnic solidarity, it's about family survival!

Democrats should champion E-Verify to protect the jobs of the more than 50 million Hispanic Americans who have the legal right to live and work here! Sixty percent of DEMOCRATIC Hispanic likely voters want mandatory E-Verify used by every U.S. employer, and 67% of Hispanics belonging to neither major party want E-Verify! This is an obvious win-win situation, and Democrats ought to find a way to compromise with Republicans in Congress to get this done. Like the Democratic Hispanic leaders along the border, national Democrats should celebrate the Border Patrol, especially since so many of its officers are Hispanic.

Some kind of "comprehensive" immigration deal could be achieved with Republicans if Democrats come to accept that Hispanics WANT border controls and relatively low immigration levels. An amnesty for many illegal aliens has been put on the table by even conservative Republicans at times in exchange for enforcement and reduced legal immigration. Stop assuming that every form of immigration enforcement is anti-Hispanic. If Democrats only want those Hispanics who believe "the government is doing too much to reduce illegal border crossings and visitor overstays," they may have to settle for the 15% of Hispanics who agree with that.

Many Democratic politicians assume Hispanics want chain migration to stay in place, but polling proves that this is a myth. Many Hispanics indeed owe their presence in the country to chain migration, but that does not mean they think this policy is good for America or should be continued.

Remember, Democrats, that Hispanics are a politically MIGRANT people, and they are not remaining static. They are assimilating into American life more every day. They, and even more their children, will not be content to be at the edges of society. They may turn as Republicans as the Italians in a few more decades if Democrats continue to misjudge their character. Lots of them may be outsiders now, but they'll be insiders tomorrow.

The destination of the political migrants

So, after all this, where are Hispanics, America's political migrants, our largest ethnic minority, heading? Of course, no one can see the future. Yet, I think there is considerable evidence that points to Hispanics voting more Republican than they ever have before in the 2022 election. Perhaps the GOP share of the Hispanic vote will reach 40% or even higher. If so, that will be a new high for a midterm election.

After that, we'll see if Democrats make the necessary adjustments to stop and reverse that trend and if Republicans seize their opportunities to continue and expand it.

APPENDIX

Hypothetical 2020 Presidential Election Outcome in Battleground States, if Hispanics had voted 45% for Pres. Trump, 55% for Pres. Biden[189]

	Georgia	Arizona	Nevada	Penn.
2020 Hispanic vote–% for Biden	62%	61%	61%	69%
2020 Hispanic vote–% for Trump	37%	37%	35%	27%
Biden's victory margin of all voters	11,779	10,457	34,000	80,555
2020 Biden victory margin among Hispanics	44,500	195,360	62,140	113,400
2020 Biden victory margin excluding Hispanic votes (Negative value indicates Biden would have lost)	-32,721	-184,903	-28,140	-32,845
2020 Biden vote among Hispanics if they had voted 45% Trump, 55% Biden	97,900	447,700	131,450	148,500
2020 Trump vote among Hispanics if they had voted 45% Trump, 55% Biden	80,100	366,300	107,550	121,500
2020 Biden margin of victory among Hispanics if they had voted 45% Trump, 55% Biden	17,800	81,400	23,900	27,000
2020 Biden margin of victory, or loss, among all voters if Hispanics had voted 45% Trump, 55% Biden. (Negative value indicates Biden would have lost.)	**-14,921**	**-103,503**	**-4,240**	**-5,845**

Notes

1 Josh A. Kraushaar, "The great realignment," *Axios*, July 14, 2022. https://www.axios.com/2022/07/14/republicans-democrats-hispnanic-voters

2 Number of 18+ Hispanics as of June, 2022, 43,824,210. Number of U.S.-born 18+ Hispanics, 23,050,545. Number of foreign-born 18+ Hispanics—20,773,665. Number of Fb 18+ Hispanic naturalized citizens, 7,991,798. Source: These numbers are based on an analysis of the June 2022 public use file of the Current Population Survey, which is collected each month by the Census Bureau for Bureau of Labor Statistics. We use the June file because it is the most recent available at the time of this writing.

3 Michael Herndon, Sonja Diaz, Bryanna Ruiz, and Natalie Masuoka, *The Power of the New Majority: A 10 State Analysis of Voters of Color in the 2020 Election* (Los Angeles, CA: UCLA Latino Policy & Politics Initiative, 2020), 6.

4 "Voting and Registration in the Election of November 2020, Current Population Survey," *U.S. Census Bureau*, April 21, 2022. https://www.census.gov/data/tables/time-series/demo/voting-and-registration/p20-585.html

5 "The Hispanic population has quadrupled in the past four decades. It is also becoming more diverse." *USA Facts*, September 24, 2021. Last modified April 18, 2022. https://usafacts.org/articles/demographics-hispanic-americans/

6 "America's Electoral Future," *The Center for American Progress*, October 19, 2020. https://www.americanprogress.org/article/americas-electoral-future-3/

7 John Anzalone, quoted by Politico staff, "Biden's pollster on the recipe for how to 'not get our a—— kicked' in the midterms," *Politico*, April 15, 2022. https://www.politico.com/news/2022/04/15/bidens-pollster-midterms-00025482

8 Kraushaar, "The great realignment."

9 Demographics are the statistical data of a population, such as age, income, education, etc.

10 John Judis and Ruy Teixeira, *The Emerging Democratic Majority* (New York, NY: Lisa Drew/Scribner, 2002), 67.

11 Ruth Igielnik, Scott Keeter and Hannah Hartig, "Behind Biden's 2020 Victory," *Pew Research Center*, June 30, 2021. https://www.pewresearch.org/politics/2021/06/30/behind-bidens-2020-victory/

12 Laura Santhanam, "Three voter trends that helped Biden," *PBS*, November 9, 2020. https://www.pbs.org/newshour/politics/3-voter-trends-that-helped-biden

13 The poll was conducted by Edison Media Research, published in "Exit polls 2012: How the vote has shifted." *The Washington Post*, November 6, 2012. https://www.washingtonpost.com/wp-srv/special/politics/2012-exit-polls/table.html

14 Edison Media Research, published in "Election 2016: Exit Polls", *The New York Times*, November 8, 2016. https://www.nytimes.com/interactive/2016/11/08/us/politics/election-exit-polls.html

15 Steven Shephard, "The Latino Population and the Latino Electorate," *Pew Research Center*, October 1, 2002. https://www.pewresearch.org/hispanic/2002/10/01/the-latino-population-and-the-latino-electorate/

16 Ruy Teixeira, "The Democrats' Hispanic Voter Problem," *The Liberal Patriot*, December 9, 2021. https://theliberalpatriot.substack.com/p/the-democrats-hispanic-voter-problem-dfc?s=r

17 Nate Cohn, "Why Trump Won: Working Class Whites," *The New York Times*, November 9, 2016. https://www.nytimes.com/2016/11/10/upshot/why-trump-won-working-class-whites.html

18 "U.S. Census Bureau Releases New Educational Attainment Data," *United States Census Bureau*, March 30, 2020, last revised October 8, 2020. https://www.census.gov/newsroom/press-releases/2020/educational-attainment.html#:~:text=%E2%80%8B

19 Steven Shepard, "New poll shows how Trump surged with women and Hispanics" — and lost anyway," *Politico*, June 30, 2021. https://www.politico.com/news/2021/06/30/new-trump-poll-women-hispanic-voters-497199

20 For example, as published in "President Exit Polls." *The New York Times*, accessed September 14, 2022. https://www.nytimes.com/elections/2012/results/president/exit-polls.html

21 Cindy Y. Rodriguez, "Latino Vote Key to Obama's Re-election," *CNN*, November 9, 2012. https://www.cnn.com/2012/11/09/politics/latino-vote-key-election/index.html

22 ibid.

23 ibid.

24 Joel Achenbach, "Zoo mystery: How did apes and birds know quake was coming?," *The Washington Post*, August 24, 2011. https://www.washingtonpost.com/national/health-science/zoo-mystery-how-did-

apes-and-birds-know-quake-was-coming/2011/08/24/gIQAZrXQcJ_
story.html

25 Jennifer Ruben, "GOP Autopsy Report Goes Bold," *The Washington
Post*, March 18, 2013. https://www.washingtonpost.com/blogs/
right-turn/wp/2013/03/18/gop-autopsy-report-goes-bold/

26 Chris Cilizza and Sean Sullivan, "Can Reince Preibys Save
the Republican Party," T*he Washington Post*, March 18, 2013.
https://www.washingtonpost.com/news/the-fix/wp/2013/03/18/
can-reince-priebus-save-the-republican-party/

27 David Corn, "SECRET VIDEO: Romney Tells Millionaire Donors
What He REALLY Thinks of Obama Voters," *Mother Jones*,
September 17, 2012.

28 The Polling Company, Inc. and WomanTrend, Nationwide Survey of
1001 likely voters, July 2014 conducted on behalf of Issues Impact
Group and NumbersUSA.

29 Sean Trende, "The Case of the Missing White Voters, Revisited,"
Real Clear Politics, June 21, 2013. https://www.realclearpolitics.
com/articles/2013/06/21/the_case_of_the_missing_white_voters_
revisited_118893.html

30 National Survey of 1,000 likely voters conducted August 8, 2013 by
Pulse Opinion Research.

31 Molly Ball, "The Unsung Architect of Trumpism," *The Atlantic
Monthly*, March 2017. https://www.theatlantic.com/politics/
archive/2017/03/kellyanne-conway-trumpism/520095/

32 "How Groups Voted in 2016," *Roper Center for Public Opinion
Research*, accessed May 22, 2022. https://ropercenter.cornell.edu/
how-groups-voted-2016

33 "How Groups Voted in 2012," *Roper Center for Public Opinion
Research*, 2022. accessed May 22, 2022. https://ropercenter.cornell.
edu/how-groups-voted-2012

34 Mark Krikorian, "New Poll: Jeff Denham's Hispanic
Constituents Don't Want His Amnesty," *National Review*,
May 18, 2018. https://www.nationalreview.com/corner/
new-poll-jeff-denhams-hispanic-constituents-dont-want-his-amnesty/

35 John Judis and Ruy Teixeira, *The Emerging Democratic Majority* (New
York, NY: Lisa Drew/Scribner, 2002), 2.

36 "Presidential Approval Ratings—George W. Bush," *Gallup*, accessed
July 2, 2022. https://news.gallup.com/poll/116500/presidential-
approval-ratings-george-bush.aspx

37 Judis and Teixeira, The Emerging Democratic Majority, 67.

38 Jonathan Stein, "Obama #1 Most Liberal Senator," *Mother Jones*,
January 1, 2008. https://www.motherjones.com/politics/2008/01/
obama-1-most-liberal-senator/

39 Barack Obama, "Address to supporters after Iowa Democratic
caucuses," as published in *New York Times*, January 3rd, 2008.

https://www.nytimes.com/2008/01/03/us/politics/03obama-transcript.
html?searchResultPosition=3

40 Sharada Dharmasankar, Bhash Mazumder, "Have Borrowers
Recovered from Foreclosures during the Great Recession?," *Federal
Reserve of Chicago*, Chicago Fed Letter No. 370, 2016. https://www.
chicagofed.org/publications/chicago-fed-letter/2016/370

41 On election day, the Democrats held 59 senate seats, including two
independents. The 60th was gained when Arlen Specter (R-PA)
switched parties.

42 Abramowitz, Alan, "The Emerging Democratic Presidential Majority:
Lessons of Obama's Victory (2013)," *APSA 2013 Annual Meeting
Paper, American Political Science Association 2013 Annual Meeting*,
August 8, 2013. https://ssrn.com/abstract=2301060

43 Jim VandeHei and Mike Allen, "The GOP's demographic decay,"
Axios, July 18, 2019. https://www.axios.com/2019/07/18/
republican-party-demographics-threat-trump-racism

44 Thomas E. Patterson, "The Republicans' demographic trap," *The
Boston Globe*, Updated July 27, 2020.

45 ibid.

46 Philip E. Wolgin and Ann Garcia, "Immigration Is Changing
the Political Landscape in Key States," *Center for American
Progress*, April 8, 2013. https://americanprogress.org/wp-content/
uploads/2013/04/ImmigrationPolitics.pdf

47 Steve Phillips, *Brown Is the New White: How the Demographic
Revolution Has Created a New American Majority*. (United States:
New Press, 2016.), *xv*

48 Ruy Teixeira, "The Democrats' Hispanic Voter Problem: More
Evidence from the 2020 Pew Validated Voter Survey," *The Liberal
Patriot*, October 7, 2021. https://theliberalpatriot.substack.com/p/
the-democrats-hispanic-voter-problem?s=r

49 Jennifer Medina, "How Democrats Missed Trump's Appeal to Latino
Voters," *New York Times*, November 9, 2020. https://www.nytimes.
com/2020/11/09/us/politics/democrats-latino-voters.html

50 The Harris Poll, "Monthly Harvard CAPS-Harris Poll: March, 2022,"
*Harvard's Center for American Political Studies and Harris Insights
and Analytics*, accessed June 1, 2022. https://harvardharrispoll.com/
crosstabs-march/ .

51 Tim Malloy and Doug Schwartz, "Biden approval hits new low amid
public discontent with both parties, Quinnipiac University national
poll finds; nearly half of Americans worry about being mass shooting
victim,"*Quinnipiac University Poll*, July 20, 2022. https://poll.qu.edu/
images/polling/us/us07202022_uazj33.pdf

52 Tim Malloy and Doug Schwartz, "Nearly 7 in 10 Favor a Limit On
How Long a SCOTUS Justice Can Serve, Quinnipiac University
National Poll Finds; 85% of Americans Expect a Recession in the Next

Year," *Quinnipiac University Poll*, May 18, 2022. https://poll.qu.edu/images/polling/us/us05182022_uirc64.pdf

53 Aaron Zitner, "Hispanic Voters Now Evenly Split Between Parties, WSJ Poll Finds," *The Wall Street Journal*, December 8, 2021. https://www.wsj.com/articles/hispanic-voters-now-evenly-split-between-parties-wsj-poll-finds-11638972769

54 Michael C. Bender, "Biden, Democrats Lose Ground on Key Issues, WSJ Poll Finds," *The Wall Street Journal*, March 11, 2022. https://www.wsj.com/articles/wsj-poll-biden-ukraine-inflation-midterms-11646975533

55 "National Tracking Poll #2204052," *Morning Consult*, April 11, 2022. https://www.politico.com/f/?id=00000180-2157-dc88-a7be-2977cac80000

56 Nate Cohn, "Poll Shows Tight Race for Control of Congress as Class Divide Widens." *The New York Times,* July 13, 2022. https://www.nytimes.com/2022/07/13/upshot/poll-2022-midterms-congress.html

57 Poll conducted April 28, 2022 to May 1, 2022 by Beacon Research and Shaw & Company Research, *Fox News*, May 3, 2022. https://static.foxnews.com/foxnews.com/content/uploads/2022/05/Fox_April-28-May-1-2022_National_Cross-Tabs_May-3-Release.pdf

58 "Survey of Texas Voters," *University of Texas at Tyler Center for Opinion Research*, May 14, 2022. https://www.uttyler.edu/politicalscience/files/dmn-uttyler-may2022.pdf.

59 Stef W. Kight, Jacque Schrag and Will Chase, "Axios midterms dashboard: What matters 2022," *Axios*, May 31, 2022. https://www.axios.com/2022/05/31/2022-midterms-election-issues-americans-google

60 "Survey of Texas Voters"

61 Geoffrey Skelley, "Biden Has Lost Support Across All Groups Of Americans — But Especially Independents And Hispanics," *FiveThirtyEight*, October 21, 2021. https://fivethirtyeight.com/features/biden-has-lost-support-across-all-groups-of-americans-but-especially-independents-and-hispanics/

62 Chart created by NumbersUSA using weekly average of polls conducted by CIVIQs, and by YouGov, January 20, 2020 to July 21, 2022. https://civiqs.com/results/approve_president_biden?annotations=true&uncertainty=true&zoomIn=true https://today.yougov.com/topics/politics/trackers/president-biden-job-approval-rating

63 Calculated by comparing data from U.S. Census Bureau with exit poll results from Edison Media Research, as published in "Election 2016: Exit Polls," *The New York Times*, accessed September 14, 2022. https://www.nytimes.com/interactive/2016/11/08/us/politics/election-exit-polls.html; "Voting and Registration in the Election of November 2020, Current Population Survey," U.S. Census Bureau, April 21,

 2022. https://www.census.gov/data/tables/time-series/demo/voting-and-registration/p20-585.html

64 Ruy Teixeira, "Confessions of a Liberal Heretic," *The New York Times*, January 25, 2022. https://www.nytimes.com/2022/01/25/us/politics/ruy-teixeira-democrats.html?smid=tw-share

65 Ruy Teixeira,"Working Class and Hispanic Voters Are Losing Interest in the Party of Abortion, Gun Control and the January 6th Hearings." *The Liberal Patriot*, July 14, 2022. https://theliberalpatriot.substack.com/p/working-class-and-hispanic-voters

66 Thomas B. Edsall, "Democrats Are Anxious About 2022 — and 2024," *The New York Times*, March 10, 2021. https://www.nytimes.com/2021/03/10/opinion/democratic-voters-anxieties.html

67 Eric Levitz, "David Shor's (Updated) 2020 Autopsy and 2022 Forecast," *New York*, March 3, 2021. https://nymag.com/intelligencer/2021/03/david-shor-2020-democrats-autopsy-hispanic-vote-midterms-trump-gop.html

68 "2020 Post-Mortem," *Equis Labs*, April 1, 2021. Slide 48. https://s3.documentcloud.org/documents/20537484/equis_post-mortem_part_one__public_deck_.pdf

69 Weiyi Cai and Ford Fessenden, "Immigrant Neighborhoods Shifted Red as the Country Chose Blue," *The New York Times*, December 20, 2020. https://www.nytimes.com/interactive/2020/12/20/us/politics/election-hispanics-asians-voting.html

70 "2020 Post Mortem," Equis Labs, Slide 24.

71 "Official 2020 Presidential General Election Results," *Federal Election Commission*, accessed June 7, 2022. https://www.fec.gov/resources/cms-content/documents/2020presgeresults.pdf All poll numbers have been rounded off to the nearest thousand.

72 "Historical Population Change Data (1910-2020)," *U.S. Census Bureau*, April 6, 2021. https://www.census.gov/data/tables/time-series/dec/popchange-data-text.html

73 "2020 Presidential General Election Results," *Federal Election Commission*, accessed June 7, 2022. https://www.fec.gov/resources/cms-content/documents/FederalElections2000_PresidentialGeneralElectionResultsbyState.pdf All poll numbers have been rounded off to the nearest thousand.

74 ibid.

75 "Net" votes means the votes for your candidate minus the votes for the other candidate. If your person gets 100 more votes than the other person, your person "nets" 100 votes.

76 See the Appendix for how these calculations were done.

77 Data from Nicholas Jones, Rachel Marks, Roberto Ramirez and Merarys Rios-Vargas, "2020 Census Illuminates Racial and Ethnic Composition of the Country," *U.S. Census Bureau*, August 12, 2021. https://www.census.gov/library/stories/2021/08/improved-race-

ethnicity-measures-reveal-united-states-population-much-more-multiracial.html

78 With the possible exception of Vikings and other seafaring traders and warriors, who established settlements as far as Greenland and perhaps on what is now the eastern shore of the U.S. around the year 1000 A.D.

79 Based on Golbez, "Map of the United States in central North America from May 21, 1840, to November 10, 1842" using Creative Commons license CC-BY SA 4.0. https://commons.wikimedia.org/wiki/File:United_States_Central_map_1840-05-21_to_1842-11-10.png (downloaded June 21, 2022).

80 David Seville Muzzy, *An American History* (Boston: Ginn and Company, 1911): 392

81 Justin Akers Chacón, *The Border Crossed Us: The Case for Opening the US-Mexico Border*, (Chicago, IL: Haymarket Books, 2021).

82 "World Population Prospects, 2022," *United Nations Department of Economic and Social Affairs, Population Division*, cited in Aaron O'Niell, "Population of Mexico from 1800 to 2020," *Statista*, June 21, 2022. https://www.statista.com/statistics/1066995/population-mexico-historical/

83 "Colonial and Pre-Federal Statistics," *United States Census Bureau.* August 2020. https://www2.census.gov/prod2/statcomp/documents/CT1970p2-13.pdf. 1168

84 Brian Gratton and Myra P. Guttman, "Hispanics in the United States: 1850-1920," *Historical Methods* Summer, 2000, 33(3) 137-153. Based on 1850 Population of Mexicans living in what are now U.S. states. http://www.latinamericanstudies.org/immigration/Hispanics-US-1850-1990.pdf

85 For ease of communication in this book, I will often use the term "Hispanic" in its modern U.S. meaning when referencing the past, even though Spanish-descent residents of those times would not have used it.

86 Martha Menchaca, *Recovering History, Constructing Race: The Indian, Black, and White Roots of Mexican Americans.* (Austin, TX, University of Texas Press. 2001). ISBN 0-292-75253-9.

87 Campbell Gibson and Kay Jung, "Historical Census Statistics on Population Totals by Race, 1790 to 1990, and by Hispanic Origin, 1970 to 1990 for the United States, Regions, Divisions, and States," *U.S. Census Bureau Population Division*, September, 2002. Accessed July 16, 2022. https://www.census.gov/content/dam/Census/library/working-papers/2002/demo/POP-twps0056.pdf

88 Jens Manuel Krogstad and Luis-Noe Bustamante, "Key facts about U.S. Latinos for National Hispanic Heritage Month," *Pew Research Center*, September 9, 2021. https://www.pewresearch.org/fact-tank/2021/09/09/key-facts-about-u-s-latinos-for-national-hispanic-heritage-month/

89 Antonio Flores, "How the U.S. Hispanic Population is Changing," *Pew Research Center*, September 18, 2017. https://www.pewresearch.org/fact-tank/2017/09/18/how-the-u-s-hispanic-population-is-changing/

90 "Population Data for Region: Rio Grande Valley," *RGV Health Connect*. https://www.rgvhealthconnect.org/demographicdata?id=281259&sectionId=935 (accessed May 17, 2022).

91 United States Department of Commerce, "About the Hispanic Population and its Origin," Census.gov, last revised April 15, 2022. https://www.census.gov/topics/population/hispanic-origin/about.html#:~:text=OMB%20defines%20%22Hispanic%20or%20Latino,or%20origin%20regardless%20of%20race.

92 Geraldo L. Cadava, "There's No Such Thing as 'the Latino Vote'," *The Atlantic*, February 14, 2022. https://www.theatlantic.com/magazine/archive/2022/03/latino-voting-history-america/621302/

93 Downloaded from "Religious Landscape Study," *Pew Research Center*, accessed May 19, 2022. Selected "Race/Ethnicity" from menu. https://www.pewresearch.org/religion/religious-landscape-study/racial-and-ethnic-composition/

94 "Profile of the Unauthorized Population: United States," *Migration Policy Institute*. https://www.migrationpolicy.org/data/unauthorized-immigrant-population/state/US (accessed May 13, 2022).

95 The Center for Immigration Studies estimates that more than 1.1 million new illegal aliens successfully arrived in the U.S. in 2021, the first year of the Biden presidency. Steven A. Camarota and Karen Ziegler, "Estimating the Illegal Immigrant Population Using the Current Population Survey," *Center for Immigration Studies*, March 29, 2022. https://cis.org/Report/Estimating-Illegal-Immigrant-Population-Using-Current-Population-Survey

96 Steven A. Camarota and Karen Ziegler, "Foreign-Born Population Hit Record 47 Million in April 2022," Center for Immigration Studies, June 1, 2022. https://cis.org/Report/ForeignBorn-Population-Hit-Record-47-Million-April-2022

97 Mark Hugo Lopez, Anna Gonzalez-Berrera and Gustavo Lopez, "Hispanic Identity Fades Across Generations as Immigrant Connections Fall Away," Pew Research Center, December 20, 2017. https://www.pewresearch.org/hispanic/2017/12/20/hispanic-identity-fades-across-generations-as-immigrant-connections-fall-away/

98 "The Hispanic population has quadrupled," *USAFacts*

99 Stella U. Ogunwole, Megan A. Rabe, Andrew W. Roberts and Zoe Caplan, "Population Under Age 18 Declined Last Decade," U.S. Census Bureau, August 12, 2021. https://www.census.gov/library/stories/2021/08/united-states-adult-population-grew-faster-than-nations-total-population-from-2010-to-2020.html

100 "2020 Profile of Older Americans," *Administration for Community Living*, May, 2021. https://acl.gov/sites/default/files/Aging%20and%20 Disability%20in%20America/2020ProfileOlderAmericans.Final_.pdf

101 Steven A. Camarota and Karen Zeigler, "Immigrant Population Hits Record 46.2 Million in November 2021," *Center for Immigration Studies*, December 20, 2021. https://cis.org/Camarota/ Immigrant-Population-Hits-Record-462-Million-November-2021

102 *USA Facts* https://data.worldbank.org/indicator/SL.UEM.TOTL.ZS

103 International Labour Organization, ILOSTAT database, as cited in "Unemployment, total (% of total labor force) (modeled ILO estimate," *The World Bank*, using data retrieved on February 8, 2022.

104 Cecilia Menjivar and Andrea Gómez Cervantes, "El Salvador: Civil War, Natural Disasters, and Gang Violence Drive Migration," *Migration Policy Institute*, August 29, 2009. https://www.migrationpolicy.org/article/el-salvador-civil-war-natural-disasters-and-gang-violence-drive-migration

105 "Forced to Flee Central America's Northern Triangle," *Medicins Sans Frontiers*, May, 2017, p. 5. https://www.msf.org/sites/msf.org/files/ msf_forced-to-flee-central-americas-northern-triangle_e.pdf

106 "Murder Rate by Country, 2022," *World Population Review*. https:// worldpopulationreview.com/country-rankings/murder-rate-by-country (accessed May 19, 2022).

107 Elisha Fieldstat, "Murder Map: Deadliest U.S. Cities," *CBS News*, updated February 23, 2022. https://www.cbsnews.com/pictures/ murder-map-deadliest-u-s-cities/

108 World Population Review

109 John F. Helliwell, Haifang Huang, Shun Wang and Max Norton, "Happiness, Benevolence, and Trust During COVID-19 and Beyond," World Happiness Report, March 18, 2022. https://worldhappiness. report/ed/2022/happiness-benevolence-and-trust-during-covid-19-and-beyond/#ranking-of-happiness-2019-2021

110 "ARCHIVE—Living Wage Series—El Salvador—September 2019—In SVC, per Month," WageIndicator Foundation. Wages shown on the website are actually in dollars, despite the label. https://wageindicator. org/salary/living-wage/archive-no-index/el-salvador-living-wage-series-september-2019 (accessed May 18, 2022).

111 "Remittances to El Salvador rebound after early pandemic drop," *Associated Press*, January 18, 2021. https://apnews.com/article/san-salvador-coronavirus-pandemic-el-salvador-1623416c0ddc7aa238911f 8a422b6c8b

112 Kevin Dubina, "Hispanics in the Labor Force: 5 Facts," *U.S. Department of Labor Blog*, September 15, 2021. https://blog.dol. gov/2021/09/15/hispanics-in-the-labor-force-5-facts

113 J. Oliver Schak and Oliver Howard Nichols, "Degree Attainment for Latino Adults: National and State Trends," *The Education Trust,* 2017. https://1k9gl1yevnfp2lpq1dhrqe17-wpengine.netdna-ssl.com/wp-content/uploads/2014/09/Latino-Degree-Attainment_FINAL_4-1.pdf (accessed June 1, 2022).

114 Organization for Economic Cooperation and Development, "Average Annual Wages," *OECD.Stat.* https://stats.oecd.org/Index.aspx?DataSetCode=AV_AN_WAGE (accessed June 21, 2022).

115 Sara Alvarez Kleinsmith, "24 Famous Hispanic Americans Who Made History," *Reader's Digest*, updated October 26, 2021. https://www.rd.com/list/hispanic-americans-who-made-history/

116 "2001 Portrait of Hispanic Active Duty Service Members," *Department of Defense Office for Diversity, Equity, and Inclusion*, Fiscal Year 2000. https://www.defense.gov/Portals/1/Spotlight/2021/national-hispanic-heritage-month/Hispanic-Infographics-2021.pdf

117 Emily Larson, "Fact Check: Are Half of All Border Patrol Agents Hispanic?" *The Daily Signal*, June 26, 2018. https://www.dailysignal.com/2018/06/26/fact-check-are-half-of-all-border-patrol-agents-hispanic/

118 Amy Norton, "Majority of U.S. Doctors No Longer White, Male," *HealthDay News*, republished July 20, 2021 by *WebMD*. https://www.webmd.com/a-to-z-guides/news/20210720/white-mens-grip-on-us-health-care-may-be-slipping

119 Richard Fry, Brian Kennedy and Cary Funk, "STEM Jobs See Uneven Progress in Increasing Gender, Racial and Ethnic Diversity," *Pew Research Center*, April 1, 2021. https://www.pewresearch.org/science/2021/04/01/stem-jobs-see-uneven-progress-in-increasing-gender-racial-and-ethnic-diversity/?utm_content=buffer8c9c5&utm_medium=social&utm_source=twitter.com&utm_campaign=buffer

120 "Treaty of Guadalupe Hidalgo [Exchange copy]; 2/2/1848," *Perfected Treaties, 1778—1945,* From General Records of the United States Government, Record Group 11; (Washington, D.C.: National Archives Building) accessed June 22, 2022. https://www.archives.gov/milestone-documents/treaty-of-guadalupe-hidalgo

121 Evans Anders, *Boss Rule in South Texas* (Austin, TX: University of Texas Press, 1982), 11

122 Gilberto Miguel Hinojosa, *A Borderlands Town in Transition* (College Station, TX: Texas A&M University Press, 1983), 97

123 Lawrence Phllip Knight, "Becoming a City and Becoming American, San Antonio, Texas, 1848-1861" *Journal of the Life and Culture of San Antonio, University of the Incarnate Word.* accessed July 14, 2022. https://www.uiw.edu/sanantonio/BecomingaCity1.html

124 "Demographic Change in Texas, 1850-2000," *The Texas Politics Project at the University of Texas at Austin*, accessed July 14, 2022.

https://texaspolitics.utexas.edu/archive/html/cult/features/0501_02/
slide2.html

125 Rogelio Saenz, "Latinos and the Changing Face of America,"
Population Reference Bureau, August 20, 2004. https://www.prb.org/
resources/latinos-and-the-changing-face-of-america/#:~:text=Over%20
the%20last%20100%20years,slightly%20more%20than%20
500%2C000%20Latinos

126 Evan Anders, *Boss Rule*

127 Jens Manuel Krogstad and Mark Hugo Lopez, "For three states, share
of Hispanic population returns to the past," *Pew Research Center*,
June 10, 2014. https://www.pewresearch.org/fact-tank/2014/06/10/
for-three-states-share-of-hispanic-population-returns-to-the-past/

128 "Overview of New Mexico Politics, 1848–1898." *History, Art &
Archives, U.S. House of Representatives*, https://history.house.gov/
Exhibitions-and-Publications/HAIC/Historical-Essays/Continental-
Expansion/New-Mexican-Politics/ (accessed June 22, 2022).

129 Robert McCaa, "Missing millions: the human cost of the Mexican
Revolution," *University of Minnesota Population Center*, accessed
June 22, 2022. https://users.pop.umn.edu/~rmccaa/missmill/mxrev.htm

130 History.com editors, "Pancho Villa attacks Columbus, New
Mexico," *History*, last updated March 8, 2021. www.history.com/
this-day-in-history/pancho-villa-attacks-columbus-new-mexico

131 Telegram from United States Ambassador Walter Page to President
Woodrow Wilson Conveying a Translation of the Zimmermann
Telegram; 2/24/1917; 862.20212 / 57 through 862.20212 / 311; Central
Decimal Files, 1910—1963; General Records of the Department of
State, Record Group 59; National Archives at College Park, College
Park, MD. Accessed June 22, 2022.
https://www.docsteach.org/documents/document/
translation-zimmermann-telegram

132 Daryll Ray, "How Did Prices Fare Following Other Golden
Ages in Agriculture," *Successful Farming*, March 25,
2015. https://www.agriculture.com/markets/analysis/corn/
how-did-prices-fare-following-or-golden_9-ar48090

133 Dick Lehr and Lee Pfeiffer, "The Birth of a Nation." *Encyclopedia
Britannica*, March 23, 2020. https://www.britannica.com/topic/
The-Birth-of-a-Nation.

134 "Basis for a Solution to the Mexican Problem," *Kourier Magazine*,
August 1926, page 25, as cited in Juan O. Sanchez, "The Ku Klux
Klan's Campaign Against Hispanics, 1921-1925." (Jefferson, NC:
McFarland & Company, 2016)

135 Juan O. Sanchez, "The Ku Klux Klan's Campaign Against Hispanics,
1921-1925." (Jefferson, NC: McFarland & Company, 2016), 30.

136 Ku Klux Klan No. 279, Records, 1921-1936, Dolph Briscoe Center for American History, the University of Texas at Austin as cited by Juan O. Sanchez, *The Ku Klux Klan Campaign*, 45.

137 Sanchez, *The Ku Klux Klan Campaign*. 226-231.

138 The Library of Congress."Depression and the Struggle for Survival : Mexican : Immigration and Relocation in U.S. History" *Classroom Materials at the Library of Congress*, accessed July 14, 2022. https://www.loc.gov/classroom-materials/immigration/mexican/depression-and-the-struggle-for-survival/.

139 Jerry Kammer, *Losing Control* (Washington, DC: Center for Immigration Studies, 2020), 29

140 "UFW History," *United Farm Workers*, accessed July 14, 2022. https://ufw.org/research/history/ufw-history/

141 Cesar Chavez to E.L. Barr, Jr., "Letter to Delano," *Farmworker Movement Documentation Project, University of California San Diego*. April 4, 1969. https://libraries.ucsd.edu/farmworkermovement/essays/essays/Letter%20From%20Delano.pdf

142 Mark Krikorian, "Cesar Chavez Belonged to a Vanishing Breed: The Pro-Borders Left," *National Review*, March 31, 2022. https://www.nationalreview.com/2022/03/cesar-chavez-belonged-to-a-vanishing-breed-the-pro-borders-left/

143 Mark Krikorian, "Yes, We Can—Make Cesar Chavez's Birthday National Border Control Day," *Center for Immigration Studies*, March 31, 2014. https://cis.org/Krikorian/Yes-We-Can-Make-Cesar-Chavezs-Birthday-National-Border-Control-Day

144 Geraldo Cadava, *The Hispanic Republican* (New York, NY: Harper Collins, 2020), 50.

145 Oscar Rosales Costaneda, "Chicano/a Movement in Washington: Timeline," *The Seattle Civil Rights and Labor History Project* Accessed July 14, 2022. https://depts.washington.edu/civilr/mecha_timeline.htm

146 "Our History," *MALDEF*, accessed July 14,2022. https://www.maldef.org/our-history/

147 Leslie Sanchez, *Los Republicanos* (New York, NY: Palgrave MacMillan, 2007), 30.

148 *Regents of the University of California v Bakke*, 438 U.S. 265 (1978).

149 Jim Norman, "Americans' Support for Affirmative Action Programs Rises," *Gallup*, February 27, 2019. https://news.gallup.com/poll/247046/americans-support-affirmative-action-programs-rises.aspx

150 Transcript of speech given at 1984 Democratic National Convention Address, San Francisco, by Jesse Jackson, July 18, 1984. *American Rhetoric*, accessed June 22, 2022. https://www.americanrhetoric.com/speeches/jessejackson1984dnc.htm

151 Maria E. Enchautegui, "Latinos and African Americans: Shared experiences, shared solutions," *Urban Institute*, May 26, 2015.

152 "How Groups Voted 2012," Roper Center.

153 History.com editors, "Nat Turner." *History*, January 26, 2021. https://
www.history.com/topics/black-history/nat-turner

154 J. David Hacker, "From '20. and odd' to 10 million: The growth of
the slave population in the United States," *Slavery Abol.* 2020; 41(4):
840–855. Published online 2020 May 13. https://www.ncbi.nlm.nih.
gov/pmc/articles/PMC7716878/

155 "Free Blacks, 1619–1860 ." *Encyclopedia of African-
American Culture and History. Encyclopedia.com.*
June 21, 2022. https://www.encyclopedia.com/history/
encyclopedias-almanacs-transcripts-and-maps/free-blacks-1619-1860

156 Kiana Cox and Christine Tamir, "Race Is Central to Identity for Black
Americans and Affects How They Connect With Each Other." *Pew
Research Center*, April 14, 2022.
https://www.pewresearch.org/race-ethnicity/2022/04/14/race-is-central-
to-identity-for-black-americans-and-affects-how-they-connect-with-
each-other/

157 Mark Hugo Lopez, Jens Manuel Krogstad and Jeffrey S. Passel, "Who
is Hispanic?" *Pew Research Center*, September 23, 2021. https://www.
pewresearch.org/fact-tank/2021/09/23/who-is-hispanic/
A 2019 survey found that 47% of Hispanics most often describe
themselves by their family's country of origin; 39% use the terms
Latino or Hispanic, and 14% most often describe themselves as
American.

158 National Geographic Society, "The Black Codes And Jim Crow Laws,"
National Geographic, last updated May 20, 2022. https://education.
nationalgeographic.org/resource/black-codes-and-jim-crow-laws

159 "Pacheco, Romualdo," *US House Of Representatives: History, Art
& Archive*, accessed July 2, 2022. https://history.house.gov/People/
detail/19284.

160 "Hernandez, Joseph Marion," *US House Of Representatives: History,
Art & Archive*s, accessed July 2, 2022. https://history.house.gov/
People/Detail/14946?ret=True.

161 "Street Fight," *POV*, filmed by Marshall Curry, PBS, 2005,
accessed July 2, 2022. http://archive.pov.org/streetfight/
black-mayors-newark-in-context/

162 William A. Galston, "New 2020 voter data: How Biden won, how
Trump kept the race close, and what it tells us about the future," *The
Brookings Institute*, July 6, 2021. https://www.brookings.edu/blog/
fixgov/2021/07/06/new-2020-voter-data-how-biden-won-how-trump-
kept-the-race-close-and-what-it-tells-us-about-the-future/

163 Dave Roos, "The Mendez Family Fought School Segregation 8 Years
Before Brown v. Board of Ed," *History*, September 18, 2019. https://
www.history.com/news/mendez-school-segregation-mexican-american

164 David Brooks, "Seven Lessons Democrats Need to Learn—Fast," *The New York Times*, April 28, 2022. https://www.nytimes.com/2022/04/28/opinion/seven-lessons-democrats-need-to-learn-fast.html.

165 "George Gallup," *Roper Center for Public Opinion Research*, 2022. https://ropercenter.cornell.edu/pioneers-polling/george-gallup.

166 Dan Casino, "How Today's Political Polling Works," *Harvard Business Review*, August 1, 2016. https://hbr.org/2016/08/how-todays-political-polling-works

167 Nate Silver, "The Death of Polling is Greatly Exaggerated." *FiveThirtyEight*, March 25, 2021.

168 "Monthly Harvard CAPS-Harris Poll: May 2022," *Harvard Center for American Political Science*, May 20, 2022. https://harvardharrispoll.com/wp-content/uploads/2022/05/May2022_HHP_Crosstabs.pdf

169 "Voting and Registration in the Election of November 2020, Current Population Survey," U.S. Census Bureau, April 21, 2022. https://www.census.gov/data/tables/time-series/demo/voting-and-registration/p20-585.html

170 "Your guide to margin of error (with calculator)," *Qualtrics*, 2022. https://www.qualtrics.com/experience-management/research/margin-of-error/ (accessed June 22, 2022)

171 "Axios/Ipsos with Telemundo U.S. Latino Survey Q2, 2022," *IPSOS*, June 18, 2022. https://www.ipsos.com/sites/default/files/ct/news/documents/2022-06/Axios%20Telemundo%20Full%20English%20Topline%20W3%2006302.pdf

172 Mark Hemingway and Ben Weingarten, "Willful Blindness: Feds Ignore Illegal Alien ID Theft Plaguing Americans as U.S. Coffers Fill," *RealClearInvestigations*, June 30, 2022. realclearinvestigations.com/articles/2022/06/29/willful_blindness_feds_ignore_massive_illegal_alien_id_theft_plaguing_americans_as_us_coffers_fill_839815.html

173 Megan Brenan, "Dissatisfaction With U.S. Immigration Level Rises to 58%," *Gallup*, February 14, 2022. https://news.gallup.com/poll/389708/dissatisfaction-immigration-level-rises.aspx

174 "Rasmussen Reports Immigration Index," *Rasmussen Reports*, July 8, 2022. https://www.rasmussenreports.com/public_content/politics/immigration_index/crosstabs_rasmussen_reports_immigration_index_july_4_7_2022

175 "Modern Immigration Wave Brings 59 Million to U.S., Driving Population Growth and Change Through 2065, Chapter 2: Immigration's Impact on Past and Future U.S. Population Change," *Pew Research Center's Hispanic Trends Project*, September 28, 2015 https://www.pewresearch.org/hispanic/2015/09/28/chapter-2-immigrations-impact-on-past-and-future-u-s-population-change/

176 "Southwest Land Border Encounters," *U.S. Customs and Border Protection*, accessed July 21, 2022. https://www.cbp.gov/newsroom/stats/southwest-land-border-encounters

177 National Survey of 1,030 likely voters conducted June, 2022 for Echelon Insights. Accessed July 15, 2022. http://60p3co1nax34ovc830mr2sak-wpengine.netdna-ssl.com/wp-content/uploads/June-2022-Omnibus-Quadrant-Crosstabs-1.pdf

178 Paul Taylor, Mark Hugo Lopez, Jessica Martinez and Gabriel Velasco, "When Labels Don't Fit: Hispanics and Their Views of Identity. Chapter 5: Politics, Values and Religion," *Pew Research Center*, April 4, 2012. https://www.pewresearch.org/hispanic/2012/04/04/v-politics-values-and-religion/?src=prc-number

179 Based on exit polls conducted by Edison Research for the National Election Pool, as cited by Jens Manuel Krogstad, Antonio Flores and Mark Hugo Lopez, "Key takeaways about Latino voters in the 2018 midterm elections," *Pew Research Center*, November 9, 2018. https://www.pewresearch.org/fact-tank/2018/11/09/how-latinos-voted-in-2018-midterms/

180 Based on exit polls conducted by Edison Research for the National Election Pool, as cited by Jens Manuel Krogstad and Mark Hugo Lopez, "Hispanic Voters in the 2014 Election," *Pew Research Center*, November 7, 2014. https://www.pewresearch.org/hispanic/2014/11/07/hispanic-voters-in-the-2014-election/

181 Jeffrey M. Jones, "U.S. Church Membership Falls Below Majority for First Time," *Gallup*, March 29, 2021. https://news.gallup.com/poll/341963/church-membership-falls-below-majority-first-time.aspx

182 Scott Bland and Elena Schneider, "New report details how Biden won 2 key states — and what Dems can learn from it," *Politico*, October 27, 2021. https://www.politico.com/news/2021/10/27/biden-key-states-report-wisconsin-nevada-517289

183 Patrick Svitek, "National Republicans zero in on South Texas congressional race to oust Vicente Gonzalez," *The Texas Tribune*, August 31, 2021. Updated September 1, 2021. https://www.texastribune.org/2021/08/31/monica-de-la-cruz-henderson-vicente-gonzalez-texas-15/

184 Maya Flores, Twitter post, July 10, 2022. https://twitter.com/MayraFlores2022/status/1546332031436656640

185 Jennider Medina, "The Rise of the Far-Right Latina," *The New York Times*, July 6, 2022.

186 Peter Aldhous and Jeremy Singer-Vine, "Which White People Support Trump?," *BuzzFeed News*, October 9, 2016, https://www.buzzfeednews.com/article/peteraldhous/trump-and-the-white-vote.

187 Carlos Odio and Rachel Stein, "2020 Post-Mortem (Part Two): The American Dream Voter," Equis Research, December 14, 2021. https://equisresearch.medium.com/post-mortem-part-two-the-american-dream-voter-66dd6f673d1e

188 Bre Payton, "ZIP Codes Didn't Imprison Democrats' Newest Socialist Candidate, Her Ideas Do," *The Federalist*,

July 3, 2018. https://thefederalist.com/2018/07/03/zip-codes-didnt-imprison-democrats-newest-socialist-candidate-ideas/

189 Calculations by author based on Hispanic turnout data from U.S. Census Bureau, "Voting and Registration in the Election of November 2020," *Census.gov*, April, 2021; and from exit poll data, "Georgia Exit Poll: President," "Arizona Exit Poll: President," "Nevada Exit Poll: President," "Pennsylvania Exit Poll: President," *ABC News*, last updated December 18, 2020.

Bibliography

Anders, Evans. *Boss Rule in South Texas*. Austin, TX: University of Texas Press, 1982.

Barretto, Matt A. *Ethnic Cues: The Role of Shared Ethnicity in Latino Political Participation*. Ann Arbor, MI: University of Michigan Press, 2010.

Beck, Roy. *Back of the Hiring Line*. Arlington, VA: NumbersUSA, 2021.

Cadava, Geraldo L. *The Hispanic Republican*. New York, NY: Harper Collins, 2020.

Carrigan, William D. and Clive Webb. *Forgotten Dead: Mob Violence against Mexicans in the United States, 1848-1928*. New York, NY: Oxford University Press, 2013.

Chacón, Justin Akers. *The Border Crossed Us: The Case for Opening the US-Mexico Border*. Chicago, IL: Haymarket Books, 2021.

Fraga, Bernard L. *The Turnout Gap: Race, Ethnicity, and Political Inequality in a Diversifying America*. New York, NY: Cambridge University Press, 2018.

Frey, William H. *Diversity Explosion: How New Racial Demographics are Remaking America*. Washington, DC: Brookings Institute Press, 2015.

Gest, Justin. *Majority Minority*. New York, NY: Oxford University Press, 2022.

Gomez, Laura E. *Inventing Latinos: A New Story of American Racism.* New York, NY: The New Press, 2020.

Herndon, Michael, Sonja Diaz, Bryanna Ruiz, and Natalie Masuoka. *The Power of the New Majority: A 10 State Analysis of Voters of Color in the 2020 Election.* Los Angeles, CA: UCLA Latino Policy & Politics Initiative, 2020.

Hinojosa, Gilberto Miguel. *A Borderlands Town in Transition.* College Station, TX: Texas A&M University Press, 1983.

Judis, John and Ruy Teixeira. *The Emerging Democratic Majority.* New York, NY: Lisa Drew/Scribner, 2002.

Kammer, Jerry. *Losing Control.* Washington, DC: Center for Immigration Studies, 2020.

Malave, Idelisse and Esti Giordani, *Latino Stats: American Hispanics by the Numbers.* New York, NY: The New Press, 2015.

Menchaca, Martha. *Recovering History, Constructing Race: The Indian, Black, and White Roots of Mexican Americans.* Austin, TX, University of Texas Press. 2001.

Muzzy, David Seville. *An American History.* Boston: Ginn and Company, 1911.

Patterson, Thomas E. *Is the Republican Party Destroying Itself?* Seattle, WA: KDP Publishing, 2022.

Phillips, Steve. *Brown Is the New White: How the Demographic Revolution Has Created a New American Majority.* United States: New Press, 2016.

Robinson, Edgar Eugene. *The Presidential Vote. 1896-1932.* Stanford, CA: Stanford University Press, 1934.

Sanchez, Juan O., *The Ku Klux Klan's Campaign Against Hispanics, 1921-1925.* Jefferson, NC: McFarland & Company, 2016.

Sanchez, Leslie. *Los Republicanos.* New York, NY: Palgrave MacMillan, 2007.

Teixeira, Ruy and Joel Rogers. *America's Forgotten Majority.* New York, NY: Basic Books, 2000.

Acknowledgments

Writing a book this steeped in polling, vote tallies and other research is of necessity long and exacting work. I could not have done it while holding down a fulltime job without the warm support and practical help of my colleagues at NumbersUSA. I want to especially thank Dan Marsh, my colleague of many years, who acted as my research assistant for this book. Dan patiently prepared footnotes, did the preliminary mining of a dozen volumes, created all the charts, and helped with copyediting.

Roy Beck, the founder of NumbersUSA, employed his decades of experience in journalism and research to pore over the text, penciling in improvement after improvement. Roy was especially helpful as a sounding board, helping me to clarify and distill my ideas. Jeremy Beck likewise gave valuable editorial insight and offered many helpful suggestions. Thanks to Thomas Redding for copyediting assistance. A big shoutout to Linda Beck, who developed the brilliant cover design.

I am grateful to Mark Mitchell of Rasmussen Reports for his patient help in developing and administering a truly innovative Hispanic survey and for helping me to interpret the results properly. Thank you, also, to the many friends and colleagues who agreed to read the text in various stages of completion.

My Hispanic friends from many countries from my old Alexandria neighborhood have a huge place in my heart, since my many years of conversation with them about politics, religion, work, and life gave me a broader and deeper sense of how Hispanics in America actually think than any pile of books could.

Lastly, I thank my family, especially my patient and supportive wife Kim, for all their wonderful help and love.

About the Author

 JIM ROBB has studied immigration trends since the 1990s. As a vice-president of NumbersUSA, Robb developed a web-based system for political activism, which has been used over 30 million times to send messages to elected officials in Washington. He has developed specialized public opinion polls to ferret out the political views of individual voting groups. Previous to policy work, Robb spent years in book and magazine publishing. He lives with his wife, Kim, in Falls Church, Virginia.